Dear Amelia and Fionn:
My First 22 Years

Suzanne Dowling

© Suzanne Dowling 2021
Published by LLM Enclosure Bay
Waiheke Island, Auckland, New Zealand
llmenclosure@gmail.com

ISBN 978-0-473-58588-4 (paperback print-on-demand)
ISBN 978-0-473-58591-4 (PDF)
ISBN 978-0-473-58589-1 (Epub)
ISBN 978-0-473-58590-7 (Kindle)

PDF edition available free via the National Library of New Zealand –
www.natlib.govt.nz
Paperback edition available as print-on-demand via Lulu – www.lulu.com
Other editions available via the publisher

Contents

Dear Amelia and Fionn:

Preface

20 October 2020

Dear Amelia and Fionn:

The purpose of the following pages is to fill in the gaps of the first **twenty-two years** of my life for your information and I hope pleasure. The onlookers in one's life can only ever know snippets as a life is a long affair, filled with momentous events and times of difficulty and struggle, but as I survey the contours of my life I look back mostly with gratitude as to the way it has unfolded especially the presence of you two in it.

As I write this I am sitting looking out at a beautiful garden in a beautiful house on the beautiful island of Waiheke Island New Zealand. Two days ago I turned 75, which is somewhat of a milestone. The Labour Government has just been re-elected with a historic landslide. There is nothing wrong with my life but it seems there is a lot wrong with the world at large. 'The time is out of joint' cried Hamlet (Hamlet Act 1, Scene 5) to reflect the dislocation of the political situation in Denmark. Many people in many countries could utter that cry as the pandemic rages almost out of control particularly in countries which are being ruled by narcissistic mad men.

Read the following pages in the spirit in which they were written, to tell you my story as best and as honestly as I can while my memories are clear, although I am cognisant of the fact that memory can be fickle. I want you to know my story up to the time I left for London to explore the world at large so that I can stop thinking about it and perhaps leave room for other outpourings which are forming an impatient queue in my mind awaiting their turn for expression. How does one unravel the tangle of a life? I really don't know. It feels like a very daunting task, but here goes!

Suzanne Dowling
Your mother and grandmother

1

Chapter 1 – In the Beginning....

Dear Amelia and Fionn:

I was born in Christchurch New Zealand on 18 October 1945, the seventh child of Isabel and Bill Dowling.

As I was the 4th girl in a row the Alleluia Chorus certainly did not break out. There were mere months between each of these four girls and we were referred to as 'steps and stairs'. There were six children under eight years of age. My father by this time was in a permanent rage at another 'bloody mouth to feed' while my mother had long since escaped into an extreme form of religion which allowed her to see the hand and will of God in everything that happened to her and led her to believe that we were all gifts from God, 'soldiers of Jesus Christ and heirs to the kingdom of Heaven'.

The nuns would always visit after a birth, oversize rosary beads clacking and clanging against the large wooden cross attached to a heavy thick leather belt around their waists (a handy tool for any corporal punishment which they may be called upon to administer). Sometimes we would announce breathlessly to my mother. 'Mother Natalie is here'. She was the head of the order and was a handsome tall, imposing woman who had Lebanese blood running in her veins which gave her a dark, attractive sultry look. This was accompanied by a low calm mellifluous voice which bespoke the presence of a authority figure to be respected and be awed by. The nuns would proceed up the hall with the threadbare carpet the 'odour of sanctity' wafting around them, glancing briefly at the new arrival before slurping a cup of tea, devouring some sweet morsel and leaving with a collective sigh of relief, happy to leave the battlefield where the 'soldiers of Jesus Christ' were slugging it out in the back room, back to their silent corridors away from the mayhem they had just witnessed.

The priest too would come to bless the child and urge an early baptism so that if the worst happened the child would not languish in limbo for all eternity. They too partook of refreshments before returning to the solitude of the presbytery and the knowledge that a fine dinner or lunch awaited them, cooked by a hirsute spinster who had the good fortune to be a priest's housekeeper, where there was a solid roof over her head, nourishing food to be prepared and consumed, and the privilege of caring for God's representatives on this earth, before she too went to her reward when her time came.

And so the Church enfolded me in its ample bosom ready to condition and programme me for my life's journey so that I too would eventually get **my** reward in Heaven as long as I went to confession regularly and erased any nasty sins especially mortal ones which could block the sight of the 'beatific vision' forever.

My mother believed in the Truby King regime of infant care. Feeds were timed for every four hours and the rest of the time the baby was trapped in a tight muslin wrap in a bassinette with the door shut against the razor-sharp bellow of the child which unless muted can cut through any heart no matter how icy. Or, when particularly pressed, she would prop the infant up on a pillow with the bottle angled to allow the flow and hurry to some other urgent task.

By the time I was born there were six children under 8 years of age. MaryClare the eldest was 11 when I was born but once Tony came along it was an avalanche of infants with a few months between each one. Rumour has it that there were also a few miscarriages along the way. There is a searing memory of one of these events. My mother was lying in the hall on an ambulance stretcher covered in blood. We were all standing around in various stages of hysterics. My father was beside himself. I clearly remember thinking that she was either dead or dying, such was her pallor. She was carted off as we all wailed loudly not knowing whether we would ever see her again. Once more no one said or explained anything so we all waited sorrowfully either to hear that she was dead or for her return which eventually happened. It was a robotic routine as it had to be but the five above me did not get much attention apart from shelter and food. Emotional needs were never considered, met or even thought of. My parents did not even know the word contraception and our family doctor was a Catholic who eventually had 11 children himself so that was a dead end.

My father was torn between his awareness of the enormity of the task which he probably thought would engulf his whole life which it did,

3

and the strong sense of responsibility which he had. All my memories of him are of his anger and even when he wasn't in a rage we were all waiting for one to burst out as they were daily events. When he drove up the drive after work there was a collective intake of breath as we waited for an explosion of some sort over something. Someone had walked on the garden. There was a dirty handprint on the garage door or the bikes had been left out in the 'bloody sun' or the 'bloody rain'.

My mother had frequent bouts of post-natal depression which saw these hapless toddlers posted off to kind and well-meaning people. We all call this 'being parked out' but this dislocation from our mother and our familiar surroundings has left emotional scars which, no matter how much therapy is embraced still endures today. Nothing was ever explained, it just happened, and we were never told when it would end. Occasionally someone came in to keep house and care for any remaining children. One such person was Mrs Metford. She came when Rolly was born and I was left at home with my father. All remaining children had been 'parked out' as far as I can recall and the house felt empty.

Mrs Metford was efficient and humourless and I have one abiding memory of her tenure. I was lying on my parents' bed during the day when she happened to come in just as I was smelling my knees. She rounded on me angrily telling me not to do this. I obeyed of course but was completely puzzled as to why this was such a heinous crime. Perhaps she perceived that I was capable of some yogic contortion which would enable me to reach my bottom and smell that. Whatever the explanation is I was old enough and had heard enough to perceive that smelling one's knees was probably a sin of impurity.

After I was born I had the good fortune to be the baby for four years. This privilege was shared only by my sister MaryClare, the eldest in the family. The explanation for the gap between MaryClare and the next child was that my father was at sea. There is an apocryphal story that my mother was alarmed by this lack of fruit and went and sat on Mother Aubert's chair in order to get something going. This is hard to believe even of my mother whose innocence and ingenuousness were legendary. Either Mother Aubert had extraordinary powers or my father came home but out they tumbled six more relentlessly year after year but stopped temporarily at me. However, after that short break came the next bunch,

4

smaller this time. They were called 'the three little ones' and came quickly with just a few months between each one. When they came along I too was 'parked out'. These memories are still quite raw, as, no matter how kind these people were I missed my mother terribly and had no idea when this exile would end. I also had no idea if my mother was ok. All I knew was that she was not home and nor was I. When she was absent there was a terrible emptiness in the house as though the life force had departed or had been sucked out leaving only a shell and a feeling of desolation. My mother was the centre of our universe and when she was not there a grey pall descended.

How they managed the gap of four years between me and the next child remains a mystery but I am told they slept in separate rooms. I was too young of course to observe this but it worked until it stopped working. Rolland, Lucy and Joseph came bouncing along to add to the chaos and my father's desperation. He was a man who liked order, cleanliness and tidiness which were in short supply in our household. His frustration was etched into his face and form and in retrospect I have a lot of sympathy for him but for me he was a person to be feared and eventually disliked because my memories and experience were never relieved by lighter moments. When people came to visit the light came on. He would joke and laugh and list our names and ages with some pride, while we looked on with solemn confusion at the sudden change. After the visitors left, the light went out and the usual dark mood descended upon the house.

My mother sunk deeper and deeper into religion. She went to mass every day and confession every week. She increasingly had a remote faraway look on her face. Later when I read Bleak House by Charles Dickens I saw similarities between my mother and the satirical character of Mrs Jellaby. This caricature has multiple children who are completely neglected as she stares into the ether thinking of the mission for needy children she is setting up in distant Africa. Meantime all around her tumble her own poor children. One constantly falls down the stairs. One gets his head firmly lodged in fence railings and several tug endlessly and fruitlessly at her skirts. Her eldest daughter who is forced to take up the slack is riddled with resentment and boiling anger as the natives of Barrieboola-Gha get the lion's share of Mrs Jellaby's attention.

5

This is of course an exaggerated view of my mother, but her obsession with the church was quite intense. Her observation of the church's tenets and strictures informed her life and therefore ours. She was forever firing money to some cause or responding to some distress signal from some dubious quarter. In a household where there was little money and for years no car, fridge or radio and a threadbare carpet lining the hall with a 'railway line' up the middle, as my father described it. So my mother's offerings to these 'causes' were indeed 'the widow's mite'.

My mother was always in a hurry which is not surprising. Even when she went to the toilet she never shut the door and always sat on the edge getting ready to spring off when the operation was complete. She did have an overactive thyroid which was eventually removed which partly explains her constant hurrying but the more convincing explanation is that she was completely overloaded on all fronts of her life. At Christmas time she would set off early in the morning with the hold all ready to fill it with things for our stockings always with head bent forward and eyes on the ground. On some occasions this paid off as she was known to find money lying on the ground. She would return to the house with the hold all bursting with gifts and hide them in her wardrobe which was not very subtle and it was known that sometimes premature peeking occurred. On Christmas eve when we were asleep and sometimes not a great deal of rustling occurred at the foot of our beds as the gifts were divvied up and put in the pillowcases tied to the foot of our beds. Already the living room was festooned with decorations across the ceiling and the Christmas tree sitting brightly in the corner. I loved Christmas and was always satisfied with what I got. Grandma O'Regan, or her agent, would despatch gifts to us from Wellington. I remember one year her present to me was a wicker basket with a lid and toggle fastenings. What I did with it I know not but I loved that basket.

Another time I received a second-hand bike which had been purchased from a family in Amesbury Street whose children had grown too big for it. How I loved that bike. On Christmas day we would all go to Mass in the morning, have our Christmas lunch with roast lamb and mint sauce. After that we played ping pong on the large table in the living room or cards or ludo. Many of these activities resulted in discord especially cards so a long and enjoyable ride around the neighbourhood dissipated any pent up competitive outbursts. Playing the piano was also a displacement activity. We had lots of books of Christmas carols which I played endlessly. We also had other music aside from a lot of classical material. One in particular was a book of the songs from Hans Christian Anderson which I loved to play. A favourite one was 'The Ugly Duckling'

> *There once was an ugly duckling. With feathers all stubby and brown. And all the other birds in so many words said #*# get out of town and #*# get out and #*# get out and #*# get out of town. So he went with a quack and a waddle and a quack, in a flurry of eiderdown.*

Of course the ugly duckling eventually turns into a beautiful swan. When Hans Christian Anderson was asked to write his biography he replied, 'I have already written it and it's called 'The Ugly Duckling'. Another favourite was *Thumbelina.*

> *Thumbelina Thumberlia tiny little thing, Thumbelina dance Thumbelina sing, Thumbelina what's the difference if you're very small. When your heart is full of love you're nine feet tall.*

There were many books containing Irish songs and I knew these off by heart and still do know many of them today. Every year there was a St Patrick's day concert on March 17th considered to be his feast day held in the church hall. I loved these concerts and the various schools participated in them mostly singing Irish songs. All sorts of people came out of the woodwork with talents they had or thought they had with pipes and violins and Irish jigs of all sorts. People played piano solos and sang solos always with an Irish theme. Everybody tried to dress in green partially or wholly.

Another diversion in our lives was the annual gala day held in the grounds of the convent. We always prayed for a fine day and put a statue of St Joseph outside in the hope of gaining some divine assistance for good weather on the big day. One of the chief attractions was the ice cream stall run by the McCarthy sisters, Eileen and Maida. They would have someone yelling over a loudspeaker 'I scream, you scream, we all scream over at Miss McCarthy's stall'. These two stalwarts of the Catholic congregation ran a cake shop not far from our house which we were sometimes allowed to patronise. They were a goodhearted pair who were always welcoming if one wandered into their shop with sixpence to spend. Another of the gala day highlights was the raffle wheel run by some loud-voiced male. One had limited spending but the gambler in me was consistently attracted to the raffles. I once won a pair of nylon stockings which delighted me a lot as I was just entering the age when this form of torture was becoming a pressing need.

Thus we amused ourselves with these annual events and in between times read the 'Lives of the Saints' several times over. I was riveted by the story of the Little Flower who washed the floors only to have her patience tried over and over again by the other nuns walking over it in muddy shoes just to test her devotion to God which of course she passed with flying colours. We also amused ourselves by trawling the neighbourhood looking for diversion and amusement which we often found in some shape or form.

Chapter 2 – Further Reflections on My Mother

Dear Amelia and Fionn:

I have already referred to my mother's constant abstraction when her mind was far away and dwelling on things which finally obsessed her and completely took over her life but during most of my childhood she was performing her motherly duties with great assiduousness. She often put on birthday parties for us, not every year but often enough to be memorable. She made special things and organised games with prizes. With our numbers this is a remarkable feat. She once remarked that her own mother was cold and to this I will add the word remote. Grandma O'Regan was not a warm person but she did add generously to our family coffers from time to time and many of us spent a lot of time at her house in Avon Street Island Bay Wellington. She was an elegant woman who was always impeccably dressed and bedecked with tasteful jewellery. My mother too, had the makings of elegance but was not very interested in bodily adornment. I have a photo of her when she was in her early fifties which attest to this possibility. Considering that she had borne ten children over a period of two decades this is remarkable.

At my grandmother's we were expected to help which was in proportion to our age. I remember going around to the butcher and collecting the gravy beef. The butcher, Mr Tillyard, was very attentive to my grandmother and only gave her the best already cut up and ready for the pot. When I stayed at Avon Street and went to school at St Madeleine Sophie's I would often sit with my grandmother in the sunporch as she took her afternoon rest. I would rub her arthritic hands and was fascinated by the elevated blood vessels in her hands which stood out like railway lines and which were soft and pliable. I would try to press them down to make them lie flat on her hand to no avail of course. I asked her if she would come back and tell me what heaven was like when she died. She said she would but of course never has. She seemed to accept this physical attention with equanimity but never returned it to me in any shape or form. This was the blueprint my mother had and she was not physically demonstrative. I have no memory of sitting on her knee or anyone's knee of even being hugged by her. I am told that I did sit on my

9

father's knee in Christchurch when the rest of the family were singing on the radio in a competition which they won. I was a few month's old. Pauline was only two but sang 'Too-Ra-Loo-Ra-Loo-Ra' very well for such a young age and I suppose it was a portend of things to come.

My mother would plant a swift kiss on our cheeks at night but that was about it. She probably felt physically overused by the time I came along so performed her motherly duties with speed and somewhat perfunctorily. She had a soft nature and never shouted at us. She simply never stuck up for herself and often looked rather forlorn as the burden of motherhood grew beyond tolerable levels. One instant stands out for me when she meekly accepted an injustice as I stood by and sadly watched. We were in a dairy near our house. This dairy was run by a woman called Mrs Brazier. She was a grumpy and unhappy woman who never smiled or uttered pleasantries. She did not walk but waddled and in retrospect I realise that she probably had bad hips which probably caused her considerable pain which would have had a bearing on her exchanges with her customers. My mother asked for an ice cream for me which was duly scooped into a cone and handed over. My mother did not have small change and gave Mrs Brazier a pound note. Mrs Brazier gave her change for a ten-shilling note. My mother told her that she had given her a pound note but Mrs Brazier refused to believe her and stuck to her guns. I think I was about four years old but I still remember the terrible pang of injustice I felt for my mother who tried to gently argue with Mrs Brazier to no avail. This was a lot of money not to have and my mother looked so dejected. As we made our way home I tentatively glanced up at her and I felt sad and saw that abstracted look and probably did not enjoy the ice cream. She was probably mentally trying to calculate other economies she could make to allow for this not inconsiderable shortfall in the coffers.

My father on the other hand was a very tactile person and was constantly trying to hug and kiss my mother who did not receive this attention with any enthusiasm. He did single out certain members of the family for his attention too but I was not one of them. Of particular note was his adoration and attention to my sister Lucy. She was a beautiful child with a lovely olive complexion, soft, slightly wavy brown hair and big soulful brown eyes. Lots of people admired her when she was a small child and gave her a lot of attention. She was even called St Maria Goretti. Sometimes she would receive his constant attention with disdain and complain that his whiskers scratched her but these objections did not deter him.

My mother was a member of the Catholic Women's League and belonged with some enthusiasm to a branch of this organisation called 'The Music Circle'. This group met monthly at one another's houses where they played and sang with great gusto. I would listen from my bed and loved to hear this as they seemed to be having a great time. Being a skilled pianist my mother played and the group sang. Sometimes they would play piano duets. They would then have supper and return to their homes. One of the members of this group was Joy Cronin who became a good friend of my mother's. She was a big woman with an authoritative air who seemed to know the answer to everything particularly when it came to knotty questions concerning faith and morals. If there was some confusion concerning fasting and receiving holy communion or eating meat on Fridays, Joy would always know the right way forward. This happened many times particularly if someone inadvertently licked a knife which had traces of marmite on it on a Friday or eleven hours before having holy communion Joy would pronounce and my mother would be content with her edict.

We called her 'The Pope'. Joy Cronin must have been a convert as her husband Bill was not a Catholic so no marriage could have taken place in the Catholic church and eternal damnation awaited her if she got married 'outside the church'. Bill Cronin was a carrier and in equal proportion to his wife's buxomness he was extremely thin and wiry. Every Sunday he would bring the family to mass in his removal truck and wait outside for the duration. Once after mass my mother was talking to this 'fount of all knowledge' when she lifted her arm to scratch her head. I was standing glued to my mother's side and saw with amazement and fascination the most voluminous bunch of hair that I had ever seen under a person's arm. It was just a glimpse until the arm returned to its normal place but was long enough to startle and perplex me. When we got home I said to my mother 'Mrs Cronin has a squirrel under her arm'. My mother's reply I do not recollect but this image stayed with me and I can see it today. At the time I think I was worried about the 'squirrel' more

11

than anything suffocating under Mrs. Cronin's arm while awaiting elevation of the arm for respiratory purposes.

My mother did not laugh much although she did have a sense of humour which sometimes manifested itself in some stock jokes which she would tell. There were two which I recall. 'Do you think I'm a little pale? No, I think you're a great big tub'. Another is a rather long one but deserving of setting out in full. A Priest had lost his voice during an important mission. In order to preach he sequestered a proxy under the pulpit to give voice to his sermon. The plan was that he whispered the words and the proxy gave full voice to them and so it began. Priest: 'Moses was an austere man' Proxy: Moses was an oysterman'....the priest let this go and continued 'He made atonement for the sins of his people' Proxy: 'he made toe ointment for the shins of his people'. Priest exasperated: 'You silly fool you've gone and spoilt it all'. Proxy: 'and the silly fool went and spilt it all'. My mother found this absolutely hilarious and so did we because she did. Presumably the mission priest marched off in high dudgeon.

When our church had its annual mission where a visiting redemptorist would come and unleash hell, fire and brimstone with fresh and terrifying reminders of what awaited us if we did not adhere unswervingly to the church's teachings and strictures. Of course they could not match the sermon on hell which James Joyce describes in 'The Portrait of an Artist as a Young Man' with the terrifying rendition of the eternal flames and in particular the infiniteness of it: 'Hell never ends. It is perpetual... Imagine a mountain of sand, a million miles high, reaching from the earth to the furthest heavens, and a million miles broad extending to the remotest space and a million miles in thickness and imagine such an enormous mass of countless particles of sand multiplied as often as there are leaves in the forest, drops of water in the mighty oceans, feathers on birds, scales on fish, hairs on animals, atoms in the vast expanse of the air and imagine that at the end of every million years a little bird came to that mountain and carried away in its beak a tiny grain of that sand. How many millions upon millions of centuries would pass before that bird had carried away even a square foot of that mountain, how many eons upon eons of ages before it had carried it all.

Yet at the end of all those billions and trillions of years eternity would have scarcely begun.'

How terrified Stephen Dedalus was as his own path had led him into a downward spiral into sin and immorality. When I read this I can glimpse where my mother's terror had its roots. She would not have read James Joyce but had listened to enough less virulent and less imaginative renditions of the terror of the eternal flames to be permanently afraid of not being in a 'state of grace' before she took her last breath.

One of the more bizarre connections my mother made was with a saintly priest in Italy called Padre Pio. He was a Capuchin monk who from a young age bore the marks of the stigmata, the wounds of Christ. How my mother knew about this man remains unclear but she probably read an article in The *Tablet*. She must have sent away for a relic and before long a bloodstained rag was to be found on her bedside table. This rag had been dipped into the wounds of Padre Pio's hands, then shipped to far away Palmerston North New Zealand. I am not clear what my mother did with these rags, but I presume she expected to get some religious updraft which would help her to get through. Recently in a church in Italy I came upon a shrine to Padre Pio and as I stood before it I thought of those bloody rags and how faith can move mountains it seems and if it can't some people believe it can.

She also had a stash of Lourdes water in her wardrobe. She possibly got these from the nuns or may have sent away for this too. This water was in small bottles and being kept in this dark place they developed slime at the bottom. If we were sick, and someone always was, she would dab this water on our heads. I remember once staunchly resisting the application to my lips, for fear I would ingest a morsel of that disgusting slime.

She subscribed to many other primitive practices of religious iconography and symbolism. We all wore Philomena cords around our waists, miraculous medals pinned to our singlets and scapulars around our necks so named as it draped over our shoulder blades which in anatomical terms is called the scapula. All these adornments were to keep us safe from harm and to ensure we were pure in thought word and deed.

Saint Philomena was the patron saint of infants, babies and youth. She was later demoted by the Vatican which only happens when the saint is not deemed saintly enough or has been outed as bogus. I put my credence on the latter. Meanwhile a tribe of children in Palmerston North New Zealand faithfully trussed themselves up in her pink platted cord sincerely believing she was the real deal. Later, when I was confirmed, my mother persuaded me to take the name Philomena as my confirmation name, which I did. The wearing of the Miraculous medal is supposed to bring special graces from the Virgin Mary and to assist in strengthening the Catholic faith in a person. My abiding memory of this medal is the observation that all our white singlets had rust stains on them from our Miraculous medals going through the wash.

The scapulars we wore were of St Francis of Assisi. The wearing of this woollen square was a guarantee that, if worn during some life-threatening misfortune, that the wearer would not suffer the eternal fires of hell. So we went about our childhood with all this iconography draped , pinned and tied giving my mother some comfort that we were protected from the dangers and temptations which were ever present even in Palmerston North.

When in fact a life threatening event did happen to me my mother was absolutely convinced that my scapular had saved me. I was 'abducted' on the way back from Mass one morning. I was riding home along Rangitikei Street when a man sidled up to me. He asked me if I wanted to come and 'see his birds'. As a child completely programmed to please adults I was very conflicted but managed to say that my parents were expecting me home and that they would be worried. 'It won't take a minute' said the man. 'Come on' He said. 'It's that house just up there with the red roof' Most houses had red roofs so I could not pinpoint which one he meant. He then took hold of my handlebars and steered me forward past the street we lived in and towards Tremaine Avenue the boundary of Palmerston North. I wasn't desperately frightened as, at this stage of my life I actually believed that adults could never do wrong and that only children were sinners and that one day I would be a sinless adult and all would be well.

As we rode I saw the familiar faces of Mr and Mrs Tottman walking along the street and looked desperately at them hoping they would look my way and sense that all was not well. They did not see me or the man. When we got to the outer edge of the built-up part of the city the man stopped and indicated to me to get over a fence. By now I was really scared by two things. The fence had barbed wire on it and I would have to navigate that without injury, but worse still there were large animals grazing in the field over the fence. They were probably steers but as a child I was scared of most animals especially big ones. The man was helping me over the fence when the eight o'clock whistle went. The man dropped me and said 'Bloody hell I'm supposed to be at work!' This was the point of that whistle. It went every day as a reminder to people that they were supposed to be at work. I do not know if every town had this whistle, but Palmerston North certainly did and it saved my life.

By this time the sense of danger had permeated. I slowly and shakily got on my bike and rode home. When I got there my mother remarked that I was late. I went into the back room and sat on my bed. Eventually my mother came in and at this stage I burst into uncontrollable sobs. As it was Saturday, my father was home and they both interrogated me. I told them what had happened having no idea of what could have befallen me or the horror of the possibilities. I do remember my father going completely berserk shouting 'I'll kill the bastard if I get my hands on him'. At his point my mother said that it was my scapular which had saved me. I was not sure what I had been saved from, and I remember wondering where the birds were and thinking that they could not be in the paddock I was being led into.

My father rang the police who came immediately. I was interrogated intensely and told my story as best I could. As a test as to my reliability they got me to name all the people in all the photos in our front room. There were lots of photos of weddings and family groups and I knew the names of every single one of those people. I passed that test with flying colours and heard them whispering to my parents out in the hall that I was trustworthy and sound and what I had told them could be relied upon. I gave a good description of the man and even today I can recall his face. Being eight years old I did not completely have the vocabulary to describe it which today I would say was sallow and hollowed out and looked very unhealthy. He had vacant grey eyes.

After that every morning before school I would be picked up by the police in a police car and driven around Palmerston North in the hope that I would spot him, but I never did. If I am honest I would say that I quite enjoyed these sojourns as I felt singled out, a rare thing in our family. This went on for three months. However, about six months later I was on the back of my brother Tony's bike going to church (which is the only thing we ever did) when I did spot him. I froze on the back of the bike and did not say a word as fear gripped me. Then a year later this man was caught having raped a child in the Esplanade. The police told my parents that I had given a very good description of the man and from that time my scapular became a firm fixture around my neck for many years to come.

A few weeks after this incident my sister Pauline and I were walking home from school when a man came up to us and said 'where do you live?' We took to our heels without a backward glance our hearts beating uncontrollably within our small chests and hurled ourselves up the drive to the safety of our house. To our horror we saw that this person was coming up the drive and knocking on the door. This turned out to be a friend of my brother Tony called Dan Finnegan from the seminary in Christchurch. He had seen us and thought that we must be Tony's sisters but for us strange men filled us with mortal terror.

So Amelia and Fionn, what an incredibly lucky escape I had. If the worst had happened I cannot help but wonder how this would have affected my life but the worst did not happen and so I have been able to live my life without that scar for which I am very grateful.

While my mother was firing off the 'widow's mite' left right and centre to all and sundry who asked for it via the pages of the Catholic Weekly *The Tablet* my father with his amazing gardening skills kept us supplied with vegetables all the year round. This must have saved a fortune. He grew onions which he would string up in the garage and filled sacks of potatoes which would last all year round. He grew cabbages as big as hot air balloons. He was pleased that in Palmerston North the lawns were small compared to the vast amount of lawn in Christchurch, which he used to describe as like 'mowing the Canterbury Plains'. He had a great compost heap and rotated his growing plan sewing lupin which he dug in to the garden for extra nourishment and was a member of New Zealand Humic Compost Club. He subscribed to their magazine called

Compost Club Magazine which illustrates his deep interest as the only other subscriptions to land in our letterbox were *The Tablet*, *The Zealandia, The Far East* and the *Marist Messenger*. The latter always had a soppy story as its feature each month.

I do not know what talentless scribe wrote these stories but they were usually dripping in sentiment. One such was a story entitled 'Sister Marie Faces the Fish'. The first line read 'Sister Marie was the youngest postulant' and went on to describe in saccharine detail the ordeal of poor Sister Marie who had to deal with some unsavoury fish as part of her trials and tribulations of 'offering things up' to God as part of her training in sisterhood. When an ordeal is looming 'Facing the fish' has become part of the vernacular in certain quarters of my family. There was a children's page in *The Tablet* which I read eagerly and sometimes sent contributions to. It was run by a person called Kathleen who I of course assumed was a woman until much later I discovered was actually a priest. I remember feeling quite cheated when this discovery was made. Through the Children's page I acquired a penfriend in Ireland called Grainne to whom I wrote often. In my head I called her Grain until I discovered much later that her name was pronounced Groinyer.

We did not appreciate my father's prodigious gardening talent until we were much older and it could possibly be claimed that our rude health both as children and adults has its genesis in my father's gardening skills. Today vegetables grown in the way my father grew them are labelled 'organic' but every morsel which passed our lips as children was 'organic'. My mother's culinary skills were at best pedestrian. She would boil cabbage in two feet of water, fry lamb's fry until it resembled the sole of a stout leather shoe and overcook cauliflower until it fell apart. There was not much damage she could do with potatoes but notwithstanding it all tasted good and we devoured it hungrily. I always loved leeks which were boiled mercilessly, but some members of the family hated them and huge uproars broke out from time to time when someone flatly refused to eat them.

By and large though, we had to eat everything put in front of us and we did. On Sundays a roast was cooked. Usually hogget roasted in several feet of dripping which was then recycled and pre-fridge days was stored in the Safe ready for the next week. The best part of the roast were the roast potatoes cooked with the hogget in the dripping. We would look on hungrily as our mother divvied them out and the competition for any leftovers was fierce. My father had made carving a roast into an art form. He could cut the slivers so thin that you could almost see through them. This roast had to last at least for another night and would be served as cold meat the next day. After that the bones would be boiled up for soup. Carving tended to send my father into a very bad temper and who can blame him? 'I'm sick of carving for millions' he would cry as he handed endless plates of meat to endless eager faces watching him at work. Now, my sympathies are all with him, but then I just thought he was the most horrible bad-tempered person on earth. We were never allowed to talk at the table so, apart from angry instructions to 'hold your knife properly' or 'take you elbows off the bloody table', silence prevailed

My Mother patiently dished up the vegetables straight from the pot in the kitchen. She made a pudding every single day. We loved her puddings and devoured them greedily. She had a set repertoire. Flummery, fruit salad and ice cream on Sundays and Junket with tinned fruit and sometimes with ice cream. Queen pudding, bread and butter pudding were other stock pieces.

On Sunday we always had whipped cream to accompany our pudding and only on that day, so when someone whipped the cream to butter and rendered it inedible there was a great hue and cry. We had had morning visitors and while they were being seen off at the gate, some unknown person had seen the beater in the cream bowl and given it a few more twists which were a few twists too many. An enquiry to rival the 'Spanish Inquisition' was launched but no one would admit to it. I was focussed on as the culprit and despite loud wailing and protestations of innocence I was locked in the bathroom until I confessed which I never did as I was innocent. The windscreen wipers almost broke down from overuse and to this day we do not know who performed those few twists but to this day I suspect my brother Dermot, who was home on one of his rare visits from the Marist Brothers' Juniorate.

My mother often made meringues and always had the 'tins filled' with biscuits, cakes and slices of various sorts. These were for us to eat but, more importantly, always ready for anyone who might drop by, especially a gaggle of nuns or a stray priest with nothing better to do.

She seldom had to go out grocery shopping as the garden supplied a great deal and in our early years there were no supermarkets. She would order by telephone from a grocery shop located at the end of our street run by a man called Mr Howard. We would hear her read out this endless list and eventually a boy would ride up the drive with a huge box on the front of his bike delivering what she had ordered. Once my brother Joseph was privy to her reading out the list when he heard her say 'Gates'. There was a long pause when she was heard to repeat that word, followed by another long pause. The she was heard to spell G A T E S Another long pause then 'Oh well Chemico will do'. The cleaning product Gates had disappeared from the market years ago and was current when she was a child. Even to this day we derive a lot of amusement from this incident as an example of my mother's vague abstraction.

Later, when we went on rare visits to Wellington or Raumati in the new shiny black Vauxhall, my mother would sometimes turn to my father when we were well on the way and say 'I think I left the jug on Bill'. Our stomachs would contract and our hearts would race as we waited for the reaction and reliably there always was one. Whether she had or not I do not recall, but those were the days before jugs turned themselves off.

The meat we ate was supplied for a long time by a man called George McKay, who would deliver it to the house. He was a jolly good-natured man and my father always cheered up no end when George turned up with the meat supply for the week. 'Are the girls laying in bed Bill?' he would say at which a cacophony of hen-like cackling noises would break out from the bedroom. We were grammar snobs from an early age led by our oldest sister MaryClare and knew that apart from in poems where poetic licence was permitted only hens laid eggs and that poor George did not know that the correct question was of course 'are the girls lying in bed'.

George, however had unwittingly 'hit the nail on the head' as our house was a bit like a hen house. One sat on a perch assigned by age. On the perch above sat the next child by age but sometimes two people particularly close in age shared a perch and pecked the person below with double strength. When Rolly became of pecking age he demonstrated at quite a young age his ambidextrous pecking skills and his nature was such that he managed to peck above (me) and below (Lucy) so double

19

pecking went on. At the top sat MaryClare the eldest, vigorously pecking Tony and Dermot. No one pecked her, this being the advantage of being the first born. I don't begrudge her this peck free life as being the eldest of 10 children was not an enviable position.

My brothers Dermot and Anthony assiduously pecked the three below but their pecking days were short-lived as each of them disappeared when they were very young. Tony went to the minor Seminary in Christchurch to train to be a priest and Dermot went to the Marist Brother's in Tuakau. Who made these decisions has never been revealed but for my mother the more vocations she could pump out of our family the better as it was fodder for the Catholic church. Dermot stayed the course and is still a member of that congregation today. My relationship with him was non- existent. I was barely five when he left home and he came home twice a year. The only strong memory is him reeking of Lane's Emulsion which repelled me.

Tony's 'vocation' did not prevail. He did his secondary schooling at the Minor Seminary in Christchurch studying Greek and Latin in which he became very proficient. He went on to study law which eventually led to a highly successful career as a legal draughtsman which is a challenging and specialised skill. His verbal utterances were always precise and refined which I suppose is a by-product of focussing every day on the precision of language ironing out any ambiguity, superfluity or wastage of words. I was barely four when he left home so for me he was a remote figure until much later in my life. Once years later, when he was employed by the Public Trust in Wellington, I met him in the street in Wellington. I was in my St. Mary's uniform complete with Panama hat and while gloves. It was like meeting a stranger who happened to be my brother. However, the connection was strong enough for him to fish in his pocket and dig out a ten-shilling note which I received with disbelief and gratitude as the only thing I could remember about him was that he had named a cat which we had had briefly. My father made it clear that a 'mob' was enough without adding a menagerie but somehow a cat managed to inveigle itself into our household. Tony named this cat Schrana. From what part of his fertile brain this name came from I do not know but Schrana it became. The cat did not survive long at all. I do not remember active cruelty but there probably was and the poor creature decided to find a more loving home and ran away.

Sunday was an important day. Mass was the highlight and of course compulsory. There was an unspoken rule that the earlier you went to mass the holier you were and much less likely to renounce your faith further down in your life. If you went to the last mass at 11am you were already a potential 'backslider' and if you sat at the back of the church at that mass you were virtually a goner. Of course a good Catholic family like us went to the earliest mass possible at 7am.

We mostly went on our bikes especially before we had a car. My father had a green work van but that was not allowed to be used for private use and he was scrupulous in adhering to this rule. We did not like this van at all. My mother walked as she could not ride a bike. I tried to teach her once, but after several tumbles into a bush I gave up. Once we had a car, a shiny black Vauxhall Velox, those who could fit in it went in that. Of course there was always our neighbour Mrs Spelman to cater for and she was a permanent fixture in our car for as long as I can remember. Sometimes we took the Tottmans who I never forgave for not seeing me as I was carted off down Rangitikei Street by the man. They had a son a priest, who eventually went on to be a bishop, so their credentials were matchless in my mother's eyes. Taking these people to mass was part of my mother's 'good works' programme.

Mrs Spelman was not popular with us. She had a scratchy voice and a mean face and never took any notice of us at all. Her lips were thin, her eyes were small and watery, the edge of her nose was always damp like a cat and she wore flaky face powder which if you sat too close to her in the back seat of the car flaked off and went on to you, so it was an unwritten competition not to be squashed next to her in the back seat. My father had no time for her and resented her lack of generosity. 'We've carted her off to church for years and she's never put so much as a mouthful of petrol in the car!' he fumed. Her meanness was amply demonstrated years later when she came down to our house during the time my mother had been consigned for many months to a mental hospital. 'Hello Sue' (a name I do not respond to but didn't waste my time enlightening her) she said with more animation than usual. 'I've brought you a bunch of battered roses and an eggless chocolate cake!'

21

That example of extreme parsimony has gone down in the annals of our family from generation to generation. She would often visit me when her domestic chores were complete and tell me with as much enthusiasm as she ever showed 'You know Sue. I've just laundered and everything is crisp and fresh'. Of course as a seventeen year old I was rivetted by such newsy tidbits.

Mrs Spelman's husband Bern was the most taciturn person I have ever encountered in my entire life. He rode a bike everywhere and how he had not been killed several times is probably more about the scarcity of traffic in Palmerston North than his biking skills. His body was so stiff that it was of a piece. In fact he looked like a cadaver on a bike. There were no moving parts except his peddling legs and the word animation could never be applied to any part of him, his body or his mind. He worked for A and T Burt in Rangitikei Street selling plumbing supplies. No doubt the taps and pipes would have sold themselves as Bern was the antithesis of a salesman.

He irritated my father beyond endurance by pedalling on the footpath from their house two doors away to our house where he would ride up the culvert onto the road. My father yelled at him on many occasions. 'Get off the bloody footpath or you'll kill one of my nippers!' I would have thought he might be grateful for a reduction in the nipper count as one of his often repeated cries was 'I'll be glad when this mob clears out'. Bern took absolutely no notice of my father's rage and continued stubbornly to mount the footpath at our gate. He was governed body and soul by his bustling wife but I witnessed him getting his own back on several occasions when he wantonly and deliberately refused to use an ashtray for his cigarette ash and directed it with some relish onto the carpet. He smoked incessantly.

During the year that I was on fulltime 'mothering' duty the three 'little ones' in a desperate bid for entertainment we would sometimes stray down to the Spelman's armed with a game which involved throwing rings onto a board which had hooks on it. This board was attached to the wall. The Spelman's seemed to enjoy playing this but I knew I had to keep a watchful eye and would sometimes accompany them. Once by some miracle Mr Spelman threw the ring and managed to score the highest point which was a thirteen. 'Thirteen Bern, thirteen' said Mrs

Spelman and thereafter this phrase entered the lexicon at least between my brother Joseph and myself when some achievement occurred. He also had a gift for saying something outrageous with a completely straight face while those around him were paralytic with the giggles. He spied a photo on the sideboard of a younger version of Mrs Spelman. She was sitting on a horse under a tree. The leaves on the tree were hanging over her head which made it look like an extension of her hair. 'What lovely hair you had as a girl Mrs Spelman'. All eyes went to the photo and muffled hysteria broke out particularly on Lucy's part as she had a tendency to giggle uncontrollably. Joseph's face was completely deadpan as he pointed at the photo. My self-control was minimal so I had to put a hasty end to the visit.

Chapter 3 – The Neighbourhood

Dear Amelia and Fionn:

After the move from Christchurch, of which I have scant memories, we lived in a three-bedroom bungalow at 35 Beresford Street in Palmerston North. I was two years old and still by some miracle the youngest. In a family our size one's childhood bons mots are seldom mentioned let alone recorded. 'Full many a flower is born to blush unseen and waste its sweetness on the desert air' said Thomas Grey in an Elegy written in a country churchyard. This is how it was, but my father often told the story of my immortal words as we boarded the interisland ferry on our way north. 'I don't want to go on the yibber' (river) said I, apparently daunted by the vastness of the ocean stretching before me which I had probably never seen before.

My father had a job with the Marine Department as a boiler and lift inspector with an area to cover which required him sometimes to travel outside the environs of Palmerston North. When he stayed overnight somewhere there was great rejoicing as we could all relax and just be with our kind benevolent but permanently distracted mother. It was always a competition as to who would sleep in her bed with her.

Our street was almost on the outskirts of the city which is not the case today as it is much more built up. Across the road from us was Central Normal School. I always pondered over why it was called 'normal' but I now know that they were schools which were intended to model best teaching practices thereby setting a standard or norm for student teachers, derived from the 16th century French concept of 'ecole normale'. Of course there was never any question that we would attend this pagan educational establishment and we were condemned eternally to walk or bike to the clutch of Catholic schools some three kilometres away. But we did take advantage of the huge playing field across the road where we played rounders on summer evenings. Later I became a friend of Susan Cowan whose father had been appointed the Headmaster there and this gave us access to the tennis court and even the key to the swimming pool on occasions.

Next to Central school was Davy Lloyd's paddock another expanse of unbuilt bare land. Davy Lloyd had a draft horse who grazed there and which its owner used to cart and carry loads of various sorts for other people. Davy Lloyd's taciturnity was second only to Bern's and I cannot ever recollect hearing him utter a single word. I never ventured into that paddock, terrified as I was of most animals, but large ones in particular. Nevertheless, without houses on the other side of the road we were not confined to a quarter acre section for our entertainment and had open spaces around which we could play and wander.

My parents would never develop relationships in the street unless the family was a Catholic family, so we were civil but distant. If there was a Catholic family nearby it was instant friendship and much toing and froing. Such was the case when the Brosnahans moved in at the back of us. They were retired farmers from Pahiatua and instantly a gate was put between their place and ours and much traffic occurred. For me they were sent from heaven as there was now a place one could go where order, tidiness, uncluttered stainless steel benches and venetian blinds reigned supreme. There were holy pictures on the wall which were surrounded by cut glass mirror frames and bliss beyond bliss they had wall to wall carpet. They never seemed to mind that we turned up regularly and for years Lucy went over there for breakfast where they dished up a nourishing bowl of porridge for her each morning. I used to go and listen to Life with Dexter and play cards and skipped over there when boredom got the better of me and none of my friends was available for distraction. Mrs Brosnahan once said to me 'do you ever walk' and I don't think I did ever walk.

Mr Brosnahan had fought in the second world war and had been shot in the knee which never worked properly for him again. Each time he took a step he had to straighten the wounded leg before he could bend it and effect movement. He was a quiet person whom one instinctively liked. One never asked questions about his infirmity but I always wondered what the story was. Mrs Brosnahan was a large buxom woman who was also kind-hearted but she certainly 'wore the trousers' and I was a bit scared of her for reasons I can't really fathom. She was very proper and upright and slightly stern. Once I went up to her and playfully tried to do 'hands knees and boomps a daisy' the last part of which requires both parties to bang each other's bottoms. To my surprise she rounded upon me angrily telling me that was very rude and I slunk home not quite knowing what I had done wrong. Sometime later Mrs Brosnahan dropped dead on the toilet and my father had to go over and carry her out. The irony of this prudish woman who disapproved of 'hands, knees and boomps a daisy' meeting such an undignified end was not lost on me even at that young age.

The Brosnahans had two daughters called Kathleen and Joan. They both did office work and Joan met her future husband Peter Coleman through her work. After the wedding there was a gathering at their house which I attended and for the first time encountered a drunk person in the form of Flossy Burns. 'Flossy is shickered' they said. I had never encountered a drunk person before let alone the word shickered and I pondered over that word for a long time. Flossy was falling over and crashing into things, which I thought was much worse than 'hand knees and boomps a daisy' but seemed to be accepted as what Flossy always did at weddings.

My father was almost a teetotaller but sometimes had a beer on Sundays and my mother had the occasional sherry. The sherry bottle was kept in their bedroom and like the Lourdes water was definitely in danger of growing things as it was so seldom drunk. We did encounter drunkenness indirectly as The Family Hotel was around the corner from where we lived and the '6 o'clock swill' was in full swing in New Zealand. We would always walk on the other side of the road if we had to go past and to this day I can recall vividly the odour of hops which emanated from there especially in summer when the windows were wide open and men stared out eyes red rimmed and bleary. I always felt frightened by the Family Hotel (a misnomer if ever there was one) especially when the roar of male voices added to the threat. Sometimes drunk men would loll about in the long grass on the fringes of Central School after dark over the road from our house. We would later find empty bottles left there and occasionally to our utter delight we found loose coins such as half a crown or a two-shilling piece and once, oh joy and rapture a ten-shilling note. When we told our mother about our finds our rapture turned to cries of disappointment and voluble objection as she

26

immediately marched us off to the local police station to hand in this booty which of course we did.

Sometimes the Brosnahans took me to church in their car, which I loved as it was clean and spacious and had no Spelman flaking face powder to watch out for. They often gave a ride to Mrs Burke whose son Doctor Burke was our family doctor and had the aforementioned eleven children. She was a very dignified and refined woman who lived in Arygyll Avenue the same street as the Brosnahan's. Once or twice I went to her house on some unknown mission and was enchanted by its spaciousness, tastefulness and quietness. It almost felt hallowed to me. There was art on the walls which wasn't kitchy stuff such as Saint Maria Goretti looking heavenward and clutching a lily the symbol of her purity and virginity which she exemplified. I cannot recall actual specific paintings as I wouldn't have known anyway but I saw for the first time art which moved one. Her house was two storied with a wide carpeted sweeping staircase leading up to further wonders which I was never privy to.

Another Catholic family moved in at the back of us and it was instant friendship. They were a young couple called Gordon and Patricia Cruden. No gate was put in as they were busy with two small children, but a stout box was put against the fence where many a conversation was had between my father and Gordon. Much later Bob and Linda Burgess moved in next door where the caravan man had been. During the Springbok tour Bob Burgess refused to play for the All Blacks on principle. He and my father would sometimes stand on a box at the fence and talk to each other. He may have assumed that my father supported the tour and was somewhat surprised and probably relieved when on one of these fence talks my father said with some vigour 'They shouldn't be letting these mongrels into the country'. As a young seaman my father had been to South Africa and was outraged to see black people step into the gutter when they encountered a white person sharing the same footpath. This made a lasting impression on him.

At the end of the street and around the corner lived the O'Donnells. Pat O'Donnell was a frequent visitor to our house and he and my father talked endlessly about Ireland and 'the troubles' and the Easter Uprising of 1916. This is a terrible history of British oppression and the Irish of my

27

father's generation absolutely hated the English with very good reason. We were never allowed to sing 'Rule Brittania' or 'God save the queen' or mention Winston Churchill's name. 'A murdering mongrel' my father would say. As soon as we saw Pat O'Donnell we all headed for the hills and considered him a tedious old bore who was completely obsessed with Ireland and the Irish. The O'Donnells had one son called Tom, who went on to be a doctor and professor of medicine of some note. I was once 'parked out' at the O'Donnell's and do not recall it being unpleasant as Mrs O'Donnell was a kind woman and I wasn't 'parked out' for long.

From time-to-time regular visitors appeared which my father loved especially if they were female. My father probably liked women more than men and he had a great sympathy for their lot. He would often be heard to speak tearfully of his mother whose life had been hard and also of other women we knew whose husbands were drunks and wastrels but who battled on regardless rearing large numbers of children with very little to come and go on. One regular visitor was Mary Bourke who was a priest's housekeeper in Fielding. She and my father would flirt mildly while my mother would make a cup of tea and bring out the biscuits.

Another visitor from an unknown source was a woman called Mrs Fitzsimons who I think was a remote cousin of ours. The absolutely noticeable thing about here was that she shaped her bright pink lipstick into a bow shape above her lips and after her cup of tea there was a terrible stain on the cup. We were highly amused by this and muffled giggles had to be stifled followed by roars of disgust after she had left as someone removed the stain. My mother wore lipstick on rare occasions and at such times made an absolute hash of applying it. She had one horrible baby pink lipstick which stayed on for about five minutes but most of the time she was far too busy to bother or care.

Yet another visitor was Ed Kavanagh. He was an amiable man who rode a bike and always clipped his trousers with a bike clip. Later he graduated to a motorised bike. He looked a bit like Sir Edmund Hilary, tall and rangy with copious amounts of hair growing out of both his nostrils and his ears. None of these people took any notice of us but I for one was taking a great deal of notice of them. There were various home helps from time to time which I suspect Grandma O'Regan paid for as my parents floundered by the sheer volume of the task they were faced with. One such person was Mrs Pedersen who lived in Wellsbourne Street which was a continuation of our street. She had several children of her own but nevertheless probably needed extra money to survive.

Mrs Pedersen was a large woman who always smelt of sandsoap. She had a least two sons whose names I never knew because she referred to them as Squibby and Tubby. She also had a daughter called Vera who we quietly renamed Popbelly as she was, like her mother very buxom. It is recounted that once Mrs Pedersen who almost took up the whole kitchen came puffing in the back door and plonked herself down on the nearest surface she could find which just happened to be the chip heater which was well alight. She leapt up as much as her bulk allowed and screeched loudly but the copiousness of her garments fortunately meant that no harm was done except the odd scorch or two.

Much later when my mother finally came back home a Mrs Ramsey came to help out. My father definitely flirted with her but this time my mother was having none of it. It was after she had had two leucotomies. Something had changed and Mrs Ramsey was sent packing. The irony is that my father was incredibly moral in these matters and when people would say flippantly 'Well Bill. I suppose you had a girl at every port when you were at sea' He would reply with some outrage. 'Of course not. I was engaged to Isabel'.

Our favourite visitors were the Lagans. They were much younger than my parents and I have no idea how they came within our radar but they did and for some time were a presence in our lives. They eventually had four children, a set of twins and two others. Margaret and Philippa always seemed to be at the Lagan's place, especially Margaret helping Kay with a family of four who were close together in age. There was never any payment for this service and it was just as well that we were all very fond of Kay who was an efficient, warm and orderly person.

Margaret felt at home at the Lagan's as there was cleanliness and order which she liked and seldom found in her own domestic environment. When she was quite young, probably in her early teens she took on the responsibility of preparing our school clothes and Sunday church clothes. We would wake up in the morning and find a neat collection of clean, ironed garments at the foot of our beds. She did this for a long time and we came to expect this I think and probably even took it for granted. It was certainly nice to see this orderly pile rather than scramble around and try to find our own garments which were probably in a disorderly pile somewhere.

One of the Lagan twins was called Bernard and he went on to become a highly respected political reporter who has worked at a multiple of venues including the *Sydney Morning Herald* and as a correspondent for *The Times*. There was one notable event that has stayed etched on my my memory. My mother would often make a batch of meringues for close friends at Christmas time and so she did one Christmas for the Lagan family. Unbeknown to her she or someone had put Alun into the container where my mother kept the sugar. Why we had alum I do not know but large quantities of it can be dangerous although it can be used in baking. So my mother made the meringues with alum instead of sugar and kindly presented the meringues to the Lagan family. How the discovery was made I know not but perhaps someone was belatedly licking the bowl or the eggbeater and tasted the bitterness so the alarm went up and the Lagans were alerted. I do not think any of the meringues had been consumed by anyone but it was considered a close call and the alum was duly consigned to the rubbish bin.

My mother had a strong habit of offering our services to other people. We would hear her on the phone say 'Ok Miss Minogue. I will send one of the girls 'round' There was an immediate flurry of escape activity. Dust flew, garments rustled as we tried to escape. Vital music practice had to be done or a game of tennis with Helen Morpeth had been arranged, but she always managed to nab someone to 'go 'round and help Miss Minogue carry in her coal scuttle. It is too heavy for her' This did not affect me so much but it definitely affected Margaret and Philippa who when the need arose happened to be just the right age to fulfil it and fulfil it they did. Another habit she had was to pick up people who were walking. There was one woman who had an ulcerated leg which emanated the foulest odour imaginable. We would beg my mother to not do this as proximity to this leg actually made us feel sick. She was always deaf to these pleas. Often she would tell us to walk if the car was too full and this command was greeted with some gratitude if 'smelly leg' was involved. If she saw a gaggle of nuns walking along we were immediately turfed out of the car regardless of the length of the journey so that the nuns could be conveyed to wherever they were going. 'You children can get out and walk' she would say.

My mother always earmarked the Catholics in our environs and we felt sorry for all the rest who we thought were destined for hell. How much we believed that is uncertain, but we were certainly programmed to believe that we were the 'saved'.

Our immediate neighbour for the entire time I lived in Palmerston North was the Hills family. They were good solid people who had a strong sense of family. Mr Hills constructed concrete driveways and other things where concrete was required. Archie Hills was a kind decent man as was his wife Ivy Hills. They had four children. Edna, George, Heather and Lois. George once tried to woo MaryClare, my eldest sister to no avail. She wasn't having a bar of an artisan who made concrete driveways as she was studying French at Victoria University and considered herself above George Hills. She did however, give him the time of day and met him at our gate from time to time. My father eventually decided to employ the services of Archie Hills and have him replace out driveway. He pulled out the flowerbeds along the side of the house and had the concrete go tight up to the edge of the house. 'A thing of beauty' he would declare proudly but with this came strictures as to egress as he was terrified that some old car would leak oil and sully this beauty. He put a chain at the gate and only cars which passed his muster were allowed up.

I can only surmise what the Hills made of us as they were unavoidably privy to the daily shouting matches and the foul language which emanated from my father's mouth but they maintained a dignified silence and acted as though they hadn't heard a thing. When a Hills child got married, which they all did, they politely invited my parents. The church at that time forbad Catholics from entering the pagan portals of another religion so attendance had to be sanctioned by the local priest.

Once the family had grown up and married and settled in Palmerston North the Hills family foregathered every Sunday at their parents' house. With almost clockwork precision after dinner they played a game of chase each other around the house. This was the most noise the Hills ever made and this practice went on for years much to our superior amusement.

Once the Hills family took a trip to Australia, which was a considerable departure from their sober ways. About a week later a large van arrived at their gate and a huge shape packed tightly in cardboard was delivered and placed on their closely cut front lawn. Once the protective cardboard was removed, a giant life size concrete kangaroo was revealed. They had made this daring purchase in Sydney. We were intrigued of course and quietly amused. They called this creature Skippy and Skippy adorned their front lawn for as long as I can remember. Mr Hills made a portable trolley on which to transport Skippy. When it rained he was wheeled into safety of their large dry garage to remain there until the weather cleared again.

Mrs Hills had a sister called Mrs Redshaw and she had hens. Every Saturday one of us had to bike to this house and collect two dozen eggs for our weekly supply. There was always an argument as to who would go and my fear was that I would fall off my bike and smash them all, the repercussions of which would have been severe. Oh well, my mother could have acquired the recipe for an 'eggless' chocolate cake from Mrs Spelman.

In general we felt superior to the Hills without any reason whatsoever. My mother once said that she thought that they probably never read books. I mopped up this remark as was my wont and the next time I went over I said 'do you read books? My mother said you probably don't'. I immediately saw that this was not the right thing to say. Mrs Hills, usually cheerful, bustly and good natured coloured markedly and snapped 'Of course we read books!' I scuttled home with my tail between my legs.

The rest of the neighbours were largely ignored by my parents but not by us. We were always looking for diversion as outings were largely non-existent due to the fact that in the early years we did not have a car and in the later years we couldn't fit into the car anyway. On the odd occasion that we did venture forth someone was usually carsick sending my father into a lather of rage and repeated exclamations of 'This is the last time I'm taking this mob anywhere' and he stayed true to his word. So entertainment on long, hot sunny weekends had to be found somewhere.

Russell Potts often filled the bill for me as he lived close by, was about my age and was willing to do daring things over at Central School. He lived with his mother and his grandmother who he called Gramma. His mother Mrs Potts worked in an office in town and every morning set off in her small Morris Minor to attend to these duties and 'bring home the bacon.' His grandmother's name was Mrs Woodruff and they lived two houses away. Russell's father had died in a car accident when Russell was very young and he was brought up by these two women in, I would say a fussy and pernickety manner. Their house was completely spotless but I only spied this from afar as was not encouraged to enter it. Perhaps they feared some cross contamination from number 35 whose standards of cleanliness could never match their own due to the insane duplications of the likes of Russell and, let's face it, they knew how messy he was.

There was something slightly unsavoury about Russell. He was certainly sneaky and had only a passing acquaintance with the truth. In short he told lies. Over at Central School amongst the trees he once took his pants off. If he thought the sight of a male organ was novel to me, then he had conveniently forgotten that I had four brothers and even at a young age, did not think this appendage was anything to enthuse over. However, I had enough of a sixth sense to hightail home rather fast and from that time stayed well clear of the bushes when Russell was around. I would surmise that Russell was gay when he reached an age to consider these things and I heard later that he ran a florist shop in Sydney.

Further along the street lived Owen Knowles. He was a much safer bet than Russell Potts. He too lived with his parents and he too was an only child. His parents were both amputees so only had two legs between them. I heard that they had met at the amputee's association. Owen Knowles was a anice boy and his parents were also kind and good to me. They sometimes took me on outings and once prior to one of these jaunts Mrs Knowles took a handkerchief from her pocket, licked it and wiped the corners of my mouth. This repelled me deeply and I vowed never to let this happen again, so I made sure that the corners of my mouth were unsullied before I ventured forth to the Knowles's house. If she showed signs of approaching with the licked handkerchief I made sure that my mouth and its corners were unavailable. I was never allowed into their house either and would always play with Owen in the yard. I never knew if this stricture was applied to all children or that I was singled out due to their fear as to the standards of hygiene of the domicile from which I had emanated.

I was also not allowed to penetrate the portals of Keith Clifford's house either. He lived further along from Owen Knowles and again was an only child. His upbringing was a closely monitored thing and he was never allowed out to play unless he had moved his bowels. His mother would say 'Keith won't be long. He just needs to do a couple'. I don't think my bowels and my mother's thoughts ever coincided so this was foreign turf (turds!!) to me but I would wait patiently. There was the odd occasion when I was sent home as the required 'couple' would not oblige and Keith could still be sitting there to this day for all I know. Keith was an easy companion and his parents were also kind and pleasant but bowel movements were certainly an obstacle to his release.

There was another couple who lived at that end of the street who had no children at all. Later, I learned that they were brother and sister. When we were consumed by boredom, we would wander into their garden and knock tentatively on the door. This activity was decidedly discouraged. They would emerge from what seemed like a very dark house and bustle us to the bottom of their stone steps. At the top of these steps stood a concrete gnome on either side. Each one had a sharp stick wedged into their hands. In retrospect I think those sticks weren't there originally and were employed to ward us off. 'If you come up the steps these gnomes will beat you with their sticks'. I completely believed them and once told this no matter how gnawed with boredom we were I would never venture up those steps. In fact after hearing this I don't think I was even prepared to go through their gate again so scared I was of those mean looking gnomes.

I sometimes wondered if my parents ever pondered on the preponderance of the phenomenon of the 'one nipper' households which prevailed in our street. It was certainly unusual and if they had thought about it, which I don't think they did, could it have given them pause to wonder? My father frequently mocked the Spelman's lack of fruitfulness while I thought it was nothing short of a miracle that they actually had one, given Bern's inertia. 'They've only got one bloody nipper, so why don't they have a car? And if they don't have a car, why don't they put some petrol in mine?' My mother certainly gave it no thought I am sure and if she did would have been derisory of such attempts at a family.

Years later when she was asking the same questions over and over again such as 'Have you been to Mass Susie?' To which I would reply 'Of Course'. 'Which church do you go to?' 'St Lukes' I would reply. She did not know that this is a shopping centre and would continue 'Who's the priest?' 'Father O'Shaunessy' I would answer so glibly that at this which point she would smell a rat and regard me quizzically. She also asked me incessantly how many children I had. 'One' I would reply decisively. She would stare at me, move her mouth around for at least 15 seconds which she did when pondering anything deep and puzzling and reply 'How did you dodge it?' How revealing is that response? I would reply 'dodging it was easy. I'd hide in the wardrobe, get under the bed, get behind the door, climb out the window, pretend I was dead.' This would send her into little paroxyms and pulsations of mirth which shook her whole body and was the most laughing I could ever get her to do and I was glad she was amused so easily.

At the other end of our street, the Rangitikei end there were two other households, the Gardens and the Pearsons. I had nothing to do with these households as they had older children. However, their presence in the street did impact on me as they both had dogs. From an early age I have always been scared of dogs. If we had had one, this may not have happened. If some brave soul ever raised the subject of adding a dog to our household my father's reply was swift and to the point 'I've got a mob. Why would I want a dog?' Even the most determined of us knew that was the deadest of ends anyone could go down, so no dog entered our household. I do not know the genesis of my dog fear. I want to believe that it's because a dog had partially bitten off the last finger of my father's left hand but, although I am hazy about this, I think this was done by some sharp instrument, possibly when he was at sea, and not by a dog at all.

The Pearson's dog was a cocker spaniel called Jip. I'm sure he was harmless, but I was terrified of Jip as he always ran out if when someone walked past. Of course he was bored. For years I could not go past their house on foot and would go right around the block along the street parallel to ours called Argyll Avenue to avoid an encounter with Jip. This added a good ten minutes to the walk home from school. Sometimes when I was feeling brave or was with someone else I would cross the road and hug the fenceline as I went past the Pearson's house. I don't think Jip ever crossed the road. I couldn't climb the fence to the safety of Davy Lloyd's paddock as there another peril awaited me in the form of his enormous drafthorse. If I was on my bike I would bike at the very edge of the road, even thrusting through the long grass, until I was out of range of that dog.

The other dog next door to Jip belonged to the Garden's and his name was Jimmy. He was a small terrier of some sort, also bored and also prone to running out to inspect passers-by. I wasn't quite so scared of him, but my fence hugging methodology and block circumnavigation served the purpose of avoiding this dog also.

So Amelia and Fionn, while the neighbourhood provided entertainment to housebound bored children it also contained perils, real or imagined. When Mrs McMurray who lived next door died and her house was sold the purchaser placed a caravan in the driveway which she let. One person to whom she let it we called 'The caravan man'. He was dubious in the extreme and was on occasions found peering into the bedroom which was only a few feet from his caravan window. No doubt he was hoping for a glimpse of a nubile female teenager of which there were one or two in our house. This meant that the curtain in this bedroom had to be permanently pulled across the window making the room semi dark all the time. There was also a man who frequented the environs of Rangitikei Street and who we were wary of. When one was walking home from school he would sidle up and mutter 'Got pants on girl?' Because he was large and inert and sprinting was out of the question for him he was not that scary and somehow we knew that 'he wasn't the full quid' as we were wont to say of such people. Nevertheless, if he did hove into view we hastily scuttled across the road to avoid him.

Chapter 4 – Flagpole Moments

Dear Amelia and Fionn:

There were in my life several times when events happened which absolutely terrified me and have stayed an abiding memory etched on my consciousness. I call these 'flagpole moments'. I am not sure why I call them that but they were occasions when the flag lying limp on its pole suddenly shot up and waved vigorously and unrelentingly because something awful had happened. This image is to illustrate how such events are sudden and unexpected. One minute all is calm and normal and the next minute there is sudden and terrifying action which renders one scared, confused and very upset with one's nervous system in overdrive. These events will crop up in this narrative from time to time and in order for you to understand their import I will give them this label.

The first such remembered event was when I lost my mother in the Palmerston North post office. One minute she was there and the next minute she had vanished. I was aged three and the only one not at school so she was the constant presence in my life during the day until the rest came back from school. Although I have described her as being emotionally absent, to me she was a constant figure who represented safety in a world which I was beginning to perceive had perils of which I was only dimly aware. She was also kind and never lost her temper or shouted. I would cling to her dress and know that all was well. Her emotional remoteness was all I knew but I do reflect now how she never picked us up or cuddled us and I have no memory of ever sitting on her knee. Perhaps she did that with the others further up the perches, but being the seventh child with six children under eight, maybe she had run out of nurturing steam. I don't think that is true. I think she was emotionally cauterised either by her own childhood or by nature. Her own mother who was distant and cold can perhaps be looked at as the blueprint for this tendency.

I ran from one end of the post office to the other crying unconsolably but there was no sign of her. People came to my aid and starting trying to help but all I wanted was the sight of her and was too distressed to speak. This is a very vivid memory and thus it is accorded the status of a 'flagpole moment'. Eventually we found each other. She had gone outside to see if I had wandered away which is why I couldn't see her in the post office itself. I have no idea how long this separation lasted but it seemed an eternity to me.

The second such moment occurred on my second day at school in February 1951. I had gone to the toilet block which was behind the school. The toilets consisted of long wooden benches each with hole in them and separated by a wall. There were four of them. Unbeknown to me these toilets operated by an automatically timed flushing system, probably every hour. I sat down and began the operation when suddenly the most terrifying explosion occurred beneath me and what felt and sounded like the Niagara Falls burst forth. There was nothing gentle about this system. It was loud and violent. I leapt off the seat and almost flew out onto the grass outside the toilets, my heart racing and my head pounding with my pants around my knees. I sat there shaking uncontrollably until I had recovered myself enough to return to the classroom. I never said a word about this to anyone and sometimes wonder if other children had such an experience.

From that day to when I went up to the next school at the age of eight I never went near those toilets again. I would go home from school constantly with wet pants and once had to do number two under a tree in Boys' High School, such was my desperation. More than once I walked home with large 'biggies' trapped in my pants but my mother never seemed to be curious as to why this child who had been perfectly toilet trained had suddenly reverted to not being so but she patiently changed my underwear without enquiry. I developed a method of pressing in my stomach when the urge to wee came upon me and this seemed to work but I often wondered if I was storing up problems for later in life. Once in primer 4 when I could not hold on any longer I went to the back of the classroom and did wees there. Richard Meech who was the class goody good and who later became a doctor and an authority on aids told on me. 'Susie Dowling has wet the floor'. Sister Sylvester, who was stern and unapproachable and should never have been allowed near small vulnerable children was always angry. She made me stay in after school and write out the times tables endlessly. How imaginative was that?

I think I cried, which is what I always did when I felt threatened. In fact after I got glasses at the age of nine the perch dwellers would all chant 'windscreen wipers' when I cried which was probably most days.

Chapter 5 – School and Education

Dear Amelia and Fionn:

I started school in February 1951. I was 5 years and 3 months old. This was an auspicious time in our history as the New Zealand waterfront strike had just begun. This was the biggest industrial confrontation in New Zealand's history. It was a flashpoint of industrial conflict whose legacy lingers today. My family were strong labour party supporters and my mother came from a very political family. Her father was the first Judge of the Court of Arbitration and the Workers' Compensation Court and before that elevation worked as a Barrister and Solicitor acting consistently for the 'working man' championing the rights of workers. He was also influential in actually shaping industrial law when he was a member of Parliament at the age of 25 standing as an independent Liberal for the Inangahua constituency.

Of course when I was five years old and embarking on that lengthy journey of education in February 1951 I had no idea about any of this but as we all grew up we were privy to political conversations and got the sense that our political loyalties lay with the dispossessed rather than the privileged. For me this loyalty is strong and prevails today as it does with all my sisters and brothers and all my nieces and nephews and now I see strong expressions of it in the next generation. As far as I know there is not one deviant at least among the members of the family who live in New Zealand whose views I have access to.

On my first day at school my mother walked me right to the gate. This was unusual as by now she had another baby and probably the next one on the way. For the most part I walked with my sisters who were at the same school, or at the next level up, the school next door. Sometimes I was dubbed on a bike by one of my sisters particularly Philippa. She would drop me at her school and I would cross the road to mine. Occasionally I was spied by Sister Margaret Mary who was serving at the tuck shop. I think she had a soft spot for me. 'Susie' she would call 'would you like a toffee bar'. Of course I never refused that treat. Sometimes my mother came to play the piano in the school hall accompanying us to the song the whole school sang every morning before going into our various classrooms. I loved it when she did this and felt proud of her. We always sang 'Little King so fair and sweet'.

Little King so fair and sweet, see us gathered at thy feet

Be thou monarch of our school,

It shall prosper 'neath thy rule

We will be thy subjects true

Brave to suffer brave to do

All our hearts to thee we bring

Take them keep them little King

The 'little king' we were singing about was The Infant of Prague whose statue apparently was responsible for some miracles and is the patron saint of children and family life.

Every morning we were met at the locked school gate by Sister Lucille who taught the 'infants' as we were called. She was a great start to my school life as she actually liked children and one got this sense quite strongly from her general demeanour. She had soft twinkly grey/blue eyes, a beautiful complexion and a gentle manner. I felt safe with her. She seemed to take a shine to me and would often say when she saw me outside the locked gate 'Thister Thuisie thewing thox for thick tholdiers' . This was because I had a pronounced lisp when I was small. I felt happily singled out, a rare thing in our lives.

I stayed in her class for primer one and two before moving next door to primer three at the age of six. Here, the honeymoon was over for the next two years. I now encountered Sister Sylvester. She was an example (and there were more to come) of a person who should never have been put in charge of little children. She was bad tempered and mean and I was terrified of her. She was an example of a nun who liked boys better than girls and there were many such instances where this was obvious. My way of dealing with nuns like her was to become good and always quiet hoping they wouldn't notice me. However, Richard Meech's tittle tattling put paid to my invisibility.

During this time we had started to prepare for our first communion which was to occur when we turned seven. The training for this huge event in our lives was Sister Colette. She had a very red face and thick glasses where her eyes were not very visible but I saw enough to be very wary of her. She was noted for making plaster of Paris statues, which were the most hideous things imaginable. She churned out hundreds of one dimensional Virgin Mary statues. The back of these statues was absolutely flat but they were handy for drawing hopscotch lines which we often did checking first that they were not 'blessed'. Many of these adorned our home.

Sister Colette's idea of 'training' was to have us parade around in a circle with our eyes closed and our hands in prayer position. This went on for hours and days and was a pretty pointless exercise as far as I can see. We dared not open our eyes or the Sister Colette's gimlet eye would bear down upon us. . We chanted the Catechism for hours on end along with the 10 Commandments and were taught the first communion hymns some of which I really liked. Sister Colette could not sing to save herself and I remember being offended by her crackly tuneless voice.

O Mary Mother sweetest best from Heaven's immortal bower,

Do gather for a little child a bouquet of sweet flowers.

I wish my little heart to be a cradle fair and gay,

where blessed Jesus may repose on my first communion day.

My little child I can obtain so bright a wreath for thee

that Jesus will delight to come within thy heart to be.

But then remember dearest child the blossoms that I bring

require the watering of a prayer or they will cease to live.

This is a kind, positive hymn and I was determined that I would 'water those blossoms' with all my might and main. Most of the other hymns were not so upbeat and resorted to the ubiquitous 'unworthy' terminology such as the following.

Oh Lord I am not worthy, to house thee in my soul
but say one word of comfort and healed my soul shall be.
When life for me is ended oh come dear lord to me.
Be with me on the journey to my true home with thee.

On the day I wore a white dress and lacy veil on my head and carried a basket filled with rose petals which at the tinkling of a bell were sprinkled about us. Receiving the communion host for the first time was a real thrill accompanied by a lurking fear that I would bite it by mistake. This was a terrible thing to do and would have to be told as soon as possible in confession as it definitely was a sin, mortal or venial I am not quite sure. As part of this milestone I made my first confession and thereafter went almost weekly to confession. All Catholics will have memories of dredging the sin box for things to confess to but there was always a reliable list which could be resorted to. I was disobedient. I told lies. I said rude words to my brother. I had impure thoughts. The very last time I went to confession was in Westminster Cathedral in London in 1968. I was twenty-two and told a mild 'sin of the flesh'. The ancient, gnarled priest turned his arthritic neck, fixed me with his beady eyes, and gave me a long penance. I stared back and realised in a flash that I would never ever go to confession again. I walked out of that cathedral and never went back. I had ditched the Catholic church forever.

When I was seven I moved up to Standard 2 where Sister Philip reigned. I think she edges into first position in the scary stakes but she did have a rival whom I later encountered in Standard 4. She was tall and thin, had white papery skin and the small glittery eyes. She never smiled, not ever. She seemed very old to me, but was probably sixty and completely unfit to teach seven-year-old children. She absolutely hammered the times tables into us and to this day I can robotically answer on any combination which has been useful over the years. She was free with the strap, but I was never on the receiving end of this humiliating practice. I was absolutely quiet and biddable and I think it helped that my mother had a sister a nun. Years later when I was in Standard 5 Sister Philip died. Her open casket was in the convent chapel and the whole school had to file past it. Luckily for me I was home sick from school that day so was spared that sight which even in my imagination scared me to death.

The playground at my first school had swings, seesaws and a field but not much else, although later a swimming pool was put at the back of the field. At playtime and lunchtime we drank the milk which had been delivered to the school that day and munched on the marmite sandwiches my mother had prepared. The tyranny of those lunches for my mother must have been relentless but we gratefully munched on them nonetheless. Fairly soon after I started school I formed friendships, some tenuous and some more enduring. It needs to be remembered that we all moved in tandem with the people we started school with, right up to the end when we left at secondary school. There were additions and departures during that time but the core group remained.

My friendships need to be the subject of a dedicated chapter but my main friend from the beginning was Joan Walters. She remained faithful and true until I departed in the 5th Form to board at St. Mary's in Wellington. I always spent lunchtime and playtime with her while other people tagged along if they felt so inclined. Helen Morpeth is in a category all of her own. She tended to bounce around between the various factions as, being highly unusual and creative, not many people 'got' her. I was always her friend as our mothers were friends and I would go to her place often outside school hours.

The playground was a bit of an ordeal at times because one had to contend with Janet Neil who 'wasn't all there' as we kindly put it. Janet Neil shouted a lot and sometimes came right up to us and roared in our faces which terrified the wits out of me. 'Fatty Castle' whose real name was Patricia was enormous and I hate to think what had happened to her in her short life as, by the age of 5 she was in an absolute rage, which caused her to threaten us with we knew not what. She often cried with rage and was always in trouble with the nuns. An alcoholic violent father was mentioned but we were far too young for enquiries of this sort and took everything we encountered at face value. Then there were the boys and while I should have been used to creatures such as these my two older brothers disappeared quite early on and hardly ever reappeared. Dermot at the age of 12 went to Tuakau to the Marist Brothers' novitiate to receive his secondary schooling and afterwards to train as a Marist

Brother, which he still is today. He came home once a year so I hardly knew him. My brother Tony had disappeared down to Christchurch to the minor seminary, where he too received his secondary schooling with a view to training as a priest afterwards. However, his 'vocation' did not endure and he left at the end of secondary school to study law. Rolly was only one when I started school and had not manifested his prodigious pecking skill at that stage so when I encountered noisy, smelly whooping boys at school I found them unpleasant.

There were two primary schools split distinctively into two buildings. One was in Carroll Street and one stayed there until the age of 7 turning 8 then moved up the following year to the other building in Fitchett Street. At the age of 12 turning 13 one went to the High School which was across the road in Fitchett Street. So having just turned 8 I migrated to the Fitchett Street school and the lovely Sister Berchmans. Finally I was away from the 'Niagara Falls' toilets and could obey the call of nature at will although in Standard 2 we could not go to the toilet if the cross was missing from the hook by the door. There were two quite heavy crosses one for the boys and one for the girls which one put around one's neck and this practice ensured that only one child was in the toilet at a time. One could speculate on the reasons for this. Perhaps it was something to do with the possibility of showing our bottoms to one another, but at this time no examination occurred as to the reason. We just did what we were told.

So Amelia and Fionn: things looked up considerably as far as school was concerned. However, sometime during that year I was sent down to Wellington because my mother was unwell. I do not know the nature of the illness but she now had ten children, the last three very close in age and the illness was mental. She was probably worn out with the domestic toil and the demands of the Catholic Church whose tenets as she interpreted them caused her incredible torment. So her children were scattered far and wide and again we were told nothing and did not even consider asking and began the long wait for her return.

I went to school at St Madeleine Sophie's and lived with my grandmother in Avon Street. I did not mind the school as my cousin Mary lived around the corner and went there too, but at my grandmother's I had to be seen and not heard so I crept about trying to cause as little trouble as

45

possible. Grandma O'Regan was very stern and hardly spoke to me but I would sit for hours as she rested either in her bedroom or in the sunporch and rub her arthritic hands. My cousins Dorothy and Isabel also lived with Grandma O'Regan. Their elder brother Tom was sometimes around but I do not remember seeing him much and believe that he was in boarding school. Isabel was a very solemn child and Dorothy being the elder of the two was efficient and organised. They were at boarding school so most of the time there was just Grandma, me and Uncle Con the father of Dorothy and Isabel. He was a kind sensitive man who always asked me questions and talked to me in an engaged gentle way. He had the rare quality of actually talking to me, in a way I was unused to in adults. Sometimes he would call on us in Palmerston North on his way back to Wellington. He would line us up, look intently at our faces and ask 'How old are you?' We would tell him and he would say 'mmmm, that deserves sixpence or a shilling', depending on how old we were. When I was staying at Avon Street he would often fish into his pocket and give me two-shillings and once half a crown, which to me was a fortune. He was rare in that generation in his kindness to us children. The other members of my mother's family tolerated us with token greetings but clearly had no interest in us at all.

Uncle Con suffered a great deal from insomnia and I would often hear him calling out in the night 'Jesus, Mary and Holy St Joseph' as he tossed and turned. He was a solicitor and partner in a Wellington firm called O'Regan, Arndt and Peters. He loved opera and sometimes sat me on his knee as he listened to Rigoletto which he loved. There I sat a bit awkwardly but not minding as it was him. I think my love of opera especially Verdi stems from those sessions with Uncle Con although later the New Zealand Opera Company came to Palmerston North. I sat spellbound listening to La Traviata and knew I wanted to hear more of this in my life. I had no idea how sad Uncle Con's life was and when I learned more about it when I was older I felt his tragedy quite profoundly and still do today. He was a notoriously bad driver and it is a miracle that he did not meet his end on the road. I drove with him and Dorothy and Isabel to Turangi, where he had a house, on more than one occasion. They would sit in the back seat staring out the back window waiting to be killed as he overtook cars on blind corners. He did have an accident once while he had a hitchhiker in the car. The hitchhiker scrambled from the wreckage and walked away leaving Uncle Con not badly injured but needing help.

There was a dog called Dinny who lived at Avon Street. Dinny was a nice dog but my phobia was still alive and well and I gave Dinny a wide berth. Once when I had let my guard down and was walking down the side of the house to the back door, Dinny came up behind me and put his paws on my shoulder. Terrified I ran into the house and shook for several minutes. Uncle Con loved Dinny . Once on one of his Turangi jaunts he opened the boot after a long 6 hour journey and out leapt poor Dinny who had jumped in the boot at Avon Street as Uncle Con was loading up the car. There was no intention of taking Dinny all that way especially squashed up in the boot.

My teacher at St Madeleine Sophie's was Miss Slattery. She was, as her name implies, rather strict and a little grim. It's a name that Dickens might have employed. She was a friend of my grandmother's and after school as I sat with her on the porch Miss Slattery would walk past and pass the time of day with my grandmother. I liked it when this happened and I think I might have been quite sycophantic as a child, but then I think the times encouraged such things as a way of gleaning small morsels of attention otherwise denied one. Years later I discovered that one of my dearest friends Randall McMullan was in the same class as me at the same school. We discovered this coincidence when somehow Miss Slattery's name cropped up and we compared notes. Randall has been an abiding presence in my life and although we were unconscious of the Miss Slattery connection at the age of 7 and 8 he is my oldest friend due to that early connection.

On Fridays the school dispensed ribbons for good behaviour. Pink was for very good behaviour and blue for good behaviour. I loved those ribbons and often came home proudly sporting one. The religious order which taught at St Madeleine Sophie's were members of the Society of the Sacred Heart (Sacre Coeur) founded by Madeleine-Sophie Barat in 1800. It may be a gross generalisation to make this claim, but they did seem by and large more appealing than the Sisters of Mercy many of whom but not all, were co-opted from the bogs of Ireland at a very young age in some cases. This would have been a grim transition for many of

47

them and who knows the private melancholy which probably informed their personalities. Of course we knew none of this and only perceived the surface manifestations of their various demeanours and were not old enough to make allowances.

It was during this time at Grandma's that I injured my arm swinging between two chairs in their front room. My cousin Dorothy took me up to Wellington hospital and it was diagnosed as a green stick fracture. It was very painful but Dorothy was so kind and good to me during this time and forever cemented in my heart a great fondness which to this day I remember keenly. She let me sleep in her bedroom with her during the early stages of my pain, rather than the grim silent quarters of my grandmother across the hall. It was also during this time that my cousin Mary O'Regan and I developed a 'crush' on Dorothy and sought her company and attention at every opportunity. We would write her notes signed 'Your devoted followers'. Later when I was a teenager Dorothy would sometimes invite me to Wellington and put me on a fuss. I would catch the Newman's bus and Dorothy would collect me from the railway station and take me out to lunch. If this wasn't treat enough she would then take me to a hairdresser where she had made an appointment for me to have my hair done. And to cap it all off she would take me to Kirkaldie and Stains and buy me two pairs of nylons which almost made me breathless with gratitude. I thought she was the kindest and best older cousin anyone could have and she certainly was. I have never forgotten her kindness to me during those years and I never will.

Dorothy was a member of the Irish Society and attended regular meetings and gatherings to which Mary was allowed to accompany her and I was not as I did not pass the strict test of Irishness. Mary's name and her luxuriant red hair were incontrovertible evidence of her ancestry and I was never sure what the criteria were as I felt pretty Irish and knew all the Irish songs off by heart, but it seems that the name Dowling did cut it and the name O'Regan did. That was a passing annoyance however, and Mary and I were firm friends and spent hours together skating up and down Avon Street and sitting on the Krause's hedge, completely going through it and probably ruining parts of it. The Krauses never ever demurred which I now find astounding and, as it was the mid-1950s, I can only put their tolerance down to their recent history about which I knew nothing, but which might have taught them 'not to sweat the small stuff' as not a single word did they say to us.

In due course I returned to Palmerston North and rejoined the ranks of standard two and Sister Berchmans. Joan Walters was faithfully waiting for me and we resumed our playground activities which largely consisted of complex ball game involving crossing our hands, throwing it behind our backs and various other contortions which are possible with a tennis ball. We sometimes played skipping which involved other people but the best bit about this school was the jungle gym. I spent hours on that jungle gym and become skilled at throwing myself around, swinging from bar to bar and catching myself by my knees and managing to land flat on my feet. This took some daring and hours of practice but that word did not define it as I loved doing it.

Sometimes I think it may be responsible for the strength of my bone structure today but that is probably 'drawing a long bow'. It was during this time that I discovered the high jump. This was situated at the back of the school field and this vied equally with the jungle gym for my attention. Because we were the youngest age group at the school we had to wait our turn to use it which often necessitated staying after school to practice. My companion in this activity was always Helen Morpeth who was a skilled high jumper. I never ever managed in the five years at that school to jump higher than she could. She won every school competition and inter-school competition and I always came second. I didn't mind and accepted her superiority in this activity unequivocally.

In Standard 2 when we were eight Helen Morpeth and I wrote a song about Joan of Arc and sang it to the tune of 'The wild Colonial Boy'. We both wrote the words but I did most of the singing as Helen Morpeth simply could not sing in tune, so she mostly mouthed the words. Sister Berchmans liked it so much she sent us into every classroom including the high school across the road to sing it. It went like this:

Saint Joan was young and brave and good and very holy too

She watched the sheep in childhood and always had work to do

She rose at dawn at 6 o'clock and began her daily tasks

A very holy girl she was and never had to be asked

49

There were two more verses involving being burned at the stake and never ever denying her religion even under the most threatening of circumstances.

And so Standard 2 merged into Standard 3 and I had just turned nine. My teacher this year was Sister Elizabeth. She seemed old to me and was a somewhat abstracted person who loved teaching us endless songs and lots of poetry. In fact that is all she did as far as I can recall. To her I give the credit of knowing the words to an array of poems and songs, the language of which enchanted me and because it did has stayed in my head all my life. 'Wait for the wagon' is one such

> *Will you come with me my Phyllis, to yon blue mountain free*
>
> *Where the blossoms smell the sweetest*
>
> *Come roll along with me*
>
> *Its' every Sunday morning when I am by your side*
>
> *So jump into the wagon and we'll all take a ride*

and

> *The Ash Grove how graceful how plainly 'tis speaking,*
>
> *the harp through it playing has language for me*

and

> *Hark Hark the Lark from Heaven's gate sings and Phoebus 'gins to rise.*

I had no idea who or what Phoebus was and had never seen an Ash Grove but it did not matter a jot as I was caught up in the poetry of it and comprehension was secondary. She never explained any of the meaning but she didn't need to. The poetry she taught us was equally bewildering

> *Oh sing as thrushes in the winter lift their ecstasy aloft amid black bows...*

and

> *by the melting drift the newborn lamb gives answer.*

It all related to a country's seasonal cycles miles from where we dwelt but analysis was never part of it and it didn't matter. I washed myself (not in the 'waters gushing from his side') but in the sound of the words and absorbed Sister Elizabeth's enthusiasm for the verbal music of the poetry.

John Gilpin was a citizen of credit and renown,

a train band captain eek was he of famous London town

was also puzzling as a 'train band captain' had thus far not crossed my path and never would!

Alone she binds and cuts the grain; and sings a melancholy strain.

Oh Listen! for the vale profound is overflowing with the sound (The Solitary Reaper by William Wordsworth)

There were other wonderful poems such as 'How they brought the good news from Ghent to Aix'

I galloped, Dirk galloped We galloped all three

and 'Kubla Khan' by Samuel Taylor Coleridge

In Xanadu did Kubla Khan,

A stately pleasure-dome decree,

Where Alph, the sacred river ran

Through caverns measureless to man,

down to the sunless sea.'

and

'Ah, what can ail thee wretched wight

Alone and palely loitering

The sedge is withered from the lake

And no birds sing

This language fed and sustained me and I would imagine 'caverns measureless to man' and the 'sunless sea' and wonder what a 'wite' was, and muse for a long time on the beauty of these words.

It was in Standard 3 when I was nine that the school did a production of Snow White and the Seven Dwarfs. Snow White was played by a girl in Standard 5 called Shona Hooker. She had lovely auburn hair and a beautiful voice. I was chosen to be one of the elves and was dressed from head to toe in a green satin outfit the top part of which was a peaked hat with a green pompom on the top. Each family was responsible for getting the costume made and somehow my mother managed to pull this off. She probably enlisted the help of Mrs Lavin who was a skilled seamstress and was a friend of my mother's. I loved being in Snow White . When Snow White came back to life as a result of the prince's kiss we sang lustily

She lives, she lives, let joyful praises ring,

let joyful praises ring.

She li-ives, she li-ives,

let joyful praises ring

Our little green pompoms bobbed and danced mirroring the delight we felt. It was another highlight of that year and I had little cognisance that it was the 'calm before the storm' of Standard 4 and Sister Clothilde when a 'flag pole' incident would occur of such strength that it has become a story passed down and eventually written about as a short story by my sister MaryClare.

I will give credit at this point to my upbringing in the appreciation of language and music. It was not just Sister Elizabeth who played a part in this, it was the Catholic Church and its rituals which were in my childhood mainly in Latin and while incomprehensible for the most part had a richness and sound quality which I loved. Again incomprehension was not a barrier to appreciation.

Et introibo adaltare dei Ad Deum qui laetificat juventutem meam.

These were the opening words of the latin Mass: I will go to the altar of God; to God who giveth joy to my youth.

Credo in unum Deum. Patrem omnipotentem factorem coeli in terrae, visibilium omnium et invisibibilium

It all sounded so mysterious and mellifluous to me as for a long time I was largely unaware that the connecting thread of this rich tapestry of words were constant barrage of reminders that we had greatly sinned and that only God in his mercy could forgive us and often with the intercession of his mother the virgin Mary. 'Mea culpa, mea culpa, mea maxima culpa' was the recurring theme..

On the other hand, the hymns we learned were largely banal and full of edifying messages depending on your gender. 'With daughters pure and sons courageous' rather sums it up and we unconsciously absorbed this unsubtle programming. There is a rare reference to the male members of the church,in the Hymn 'I'll sing a hymn to Mary' with the line 'when wicked men blaspheme thee, I'll love and bless thy name' This refers to the collective human race of course and as far as I can recall instructional messages to the male members of the church were almost non-existent. The imagery of many of the hymns except the ones about the Virgin Mary was gruesome and macabre.

By the blood which flowed from thee in thy grievous agony'

and

'blood of my saviour bathe me in thy tide,

wash me ye waters gushing from thy side'

and

deep in thy wounds lord hide and shelter me.

Thus we sang about this bodily carnage with great enthusiasm and there was absolutely no censorship rating for small vulnerable children who might be a little unsettled by the mental pictures which being 'hidden in wounds' might gave rise to. Who wrote these hymns I do not know but possibly some lonely monk in a cold cell where bodily comforts were hard to come by and mortification of the flesh was the daily diet and whose main aim in life was to inflict his morbid fancies on many generations to come. We also used to say this prayer on Good Friday which, if dwelt upon, was a low point in ghoulishness. Every verse began with the words 'I kiss the wounds' and went through the whole of Christ's body for five verses, Sacred head, sacred feet, sacred hands, sacred shoulder and finally sacred heart.

The hymns about the Virgin Mary were always sentimental and promoted virginity at every turn 'The virgin of all virgins of David's royal blood' and 'the one spotless womb wherein Jesus was laid' and 'Oh gentle chaste and spotless maid'. But then virginity was the recurring themes of our upbringing so imagine the shame when a breach occurred and a young teenage girl had to be whisked off to some remote farm to eek out the time of gestation while her embarrassed and ashamed parents fabricated stories about why this girl had disappeared, which of course no one believed. 'Woe betide' any girl whose womb ceased to be spotless and became sullied. A remote farm in the Wairarapa was her just deserts. She might even have been a member of 'The children of Mary' a lay society in the church which young teenage girls were encouraged to join and of course we all did.

This society met every month at a Sunday Mass. We were all dressed in a long blue robe with a white veil over our heads looking just like the Virgin Mary with a miraculous medal on a blue ribbon around our neck transferred temporarily from our singlet for the occasion. After the Mass we met and chanted what was called 'The office of the Children of Mary'. None of this has stayed in my head except one memorable line 'As David was nursed in fair Abishag's breast'. Apparently this paragon was a beautiful young girl who assisted King David in his decline by lying in his bosom and keeping him warm. It is claimed that no further intimacies occurred but one cannot help but be amused in this modern age by the name Abi**SHAG** with its implications as to other possibilities.

My mother lived in mortal fear that one of us would become pregnant and she was particularly worried about Margaret and Pauline both of whom were attractive and a magnet for boys. When Margaret would be dropped off at night after an outing with one of her boyfriends she would always see the curtain twitch in my mother's bedroom as she peered out in order to stop 'an occasion of sin' in its tracks. Pauline too had to be reined in for fear that she would become a widgy and that her frequenting of the Broadway Milkbar to see boys would be her undoing. The solution was to send her to St Mary's in Wellington to boarding school. This proved to be a good thing but possibly for the wrong reasons. She flourished musically there in the hands of Sister Loretto as I have already recounted. Fortunately there was not such an establishment as the 'Magdalene Laundries' in New Zealand for young women who were labelled as 'fallen' and is the subject of that 2002 film about such a place in Ireland. Had Margaret or Pauline 'fallen' we have no doubt that, had there been such a place in New Zealand they would have been sent there as my mother had an absolute naive belief in the holiness and goodness of anyone who wore a habit, dog collar or biretta.

Sometimes, I thought, she was not of this world not just because of her extreme religiosity but also because she had some strange beliefs to which she adhered tenaciously. She thought that crossed knives were a definite sign of impending discord. That, after an egg is boiled the pots must be washed thoroughly as there is something in the egg which stays and contaminates the pot. I have always struggled with these two things and I too uncross knives and wash a pot thoroughly after an egg has been boiled in it. Once when I gave her *The Guinness Book of Records* for Christmas, a rather lame present but one which I thought might entertain her, she turned to me with a slightly troubled look and said 'But Susie, we haven't got a record player!'

Boyfriend candidates were not lining up for me unless one can count sitting on Russell Finnerty's knee in the car after a dance can be counted. It is more likely that there was not there was not enough room in the car. Later however, a boy called Noel Hughes gave me some attention. He played the violin and he knew that I played the piano but soon discovered that I was not quite good enough for piano/violin duos and, after several refusals to go to the pictures, he gave up. Later he became the first violin in the Sydney Symphony Orchestra so I puzzled on that possibility had I given it oxygen. Then there was David Kinniburgh who had parents in Palmerston North and on several occasions gave me a ride back to Wellington, where he also lived, in his Vintage car. There was great amazement as he drew up at Beresford Street to collect me.

All the hymns spoke of our unworthiness our sinfulness, our worthlessness, our guilt and the unlikelihood of getting 'up there' eventually unless we absolutely and completely obeyed every stricture the church put upon us. More importantly our timing had to be on the button as to enter Heaven we had to be in 'state of grace' so if one had an impure thought, then got knocked off one's bike it was purgatory for as long as it took to cleanse us to be worthy of the 'beatific vision'. No wonder my mother lived in a state of abject terror that she might be caught short by some senseless bad luck and drop dead with an unconfessed sin on her soul. She went to confession every single week, staying in the confessional for an embarrassing length of time and speaking in a stage whisper while we cringed outside pretending that we had absolutely no connection to her. She was so afraid of forgetting something and trawled the mire of the sin bank for every possible transgression so that she could sleep easy with a clean slate and with any luck 'be taken' while in that state.

Before long however, she felt the creeping return of those stains on her soul and her anxiety returned in full strength. I have no idea why she was like this and what gave rise to this painful state of mind. She constantly reminded us that 'we know not the day nor the hour, for death will come like a thief in the night when we least expect it'. Every night as we lay down to rest we would be told to cross our arms over our chest and say 'I must die. I know not when nor how nor when. But if I die in mortal sin I will be lost forever. Sweet Jesus have mercy on my soul. Mary help me' Every night we knelt beside our beds to say our night prayers which my mother had composed long ago to cover all contingencies 'God bless mum and dad, my brothers and sisters, grandma and granddad and all my relations living dead and sick. God bless Mrs Knox and Olive, Sister Fidelma, Daisy Gordon, Ina, Mrs Burgess and Aunty Cis' . I may have missed some people out as it was quite a list and as one got older one puzzled over who the unknown people were.

Sister Fidelma had delivered most of us at Beckenham hospital in Christchurch. Ina was the secretary assistant to a lawyer they knew called Mr Amodeo. She was a non-Catholic and it was hoped that the cumulative effect of these prayers might by osmosis draw her towards converting. As far as I know it did not happen. I'm not sure about Daisy Gordon but Mrs Burgess had got divorced which, in my mother's eyes was a terrible sin, and condemned the poor woman to the eternal flames. As far as I know Mrs Burgess was also unconscious of the considerable energy being expended in Palmerston North to saving her from this horrible fate.

Aunty Cis however, was a real presence in our lives. Her relationship to us I have to declare I am vague about but her real name was Hannah Fogarty and had married into some branch of the O'Regan clan and was I think my mother's cousin. She had no children and had developed terrible arthritis which rendered her almost unable to walk and when she did it was a slow and painful action. She was a brave and stoical woman and I never heard her complain although she must have been in considerable pain a lot of the time. She lived in Wellington with her niece Clare Leydon and her husband Barney. Once a year she was despatched to our house for a month to give her niece a break. To this day I do not know how all these people were accommodated but she always slept in what we called the side room sharing it with some other member of the family. Presumably the ousted occupant was shunted to what we called the back room to join the other five already in residence. During the year my mother saved up all the darning for Aunty Cis who systematically went through it and darned endless socks and jerseys with her intensely arthritic hands. She must have become immune to the family eruptions and she came back year after year. The priest would breeze in every week to give her communion.

As to confession I am not sure how that was dealt with but there might have been some whisperings in the side room from time to time. What possible sins Auntie Cis could have committed is hard to imagine but she may have had impure thoughts or might have cursed my father under her breath as he rampaged about. She sat in the corner of the living room darning and sometimes got very anxious during the bedtime routine as we flagrantly disobeyed my mother as she set about corralling us to bed. Occasionally she would make an utterance about doing the dishes which we all avoided like the plague. This is the only time my kind and patient mother sometimes showed vexation and occasionally picked up a coat hanger to threaten us but it never seemed to be applied to our flesh.

Chapter 6 – When I was Seven

Dear Amelia and Fionn:

At this point I want to tell you about the year I was seven as it was an eventful year. There was Sister Phillip and I made my first communion. I had my tonsils and adenoids out and 'The China Horse' episode occurred.

I have already talked about my First Communion and Sister Phillip so now I will tell you about having my tonsils and adenoids out. I have no idea what led to this but no doubt Doctor Burke decreed that it was necessary. It was decided that I should be sent to the Home of Compassion in Island Bay as my family had strong connections with this establishment. As mentioned already, my grandmother was a friend of Suzanne Aubert the founder and of course I am called after her. My uncle, Rolland O'Regan operated there once a week for no fee. I was put in ward which was completely empty. My bed was in the corner near the door. The operation was carried out and my strongest memories are of considerable pain and general feeling of abandonment but there was also copious amounts of ice cream and jelly which softened the blow.

After the operation there was a complication as the bleeding would not stop, so I was carted back into the operating theatre to staunch the flow. More pain and misery and during this procedure I had a really horrible dream or sensation of a bubble going along a pipe and making a horrible ethereal, echoey sound which was horrible and strangely threatening. I had lots of visitors from the nuns who lived at the Home of Compassion and the stock question always was. 'What are you going to be when you grow up?' By then I had made sycophancy into an art form and my stock reply was 'I am going to be a Sister of Compassion' This was of course the right answer and was met with great approval. The only other visitor was Aunty Cassie. She came on several occasions and to this day I am eternally grateful to her. By this time she had five children of her own and was a busy person. I was oblivious to this of course and only reflected much later how kind she was to come and see me. My grandmother never darkened the door but as she did not drive a car it may have been difficult for her. But I do not think it even occurred to her that visiting a sick grandchild, far from home might have been a good thing to do, especially as she lived about half a kilometre away. Uncle Ro popped his head in, smiled benevolently, made some patronising remarks while the nuns buzzed around him adulating the great surgeon. I uttered not a single word but then the visit was so fleeting as he had more pressing business in the operating theatre.

The 'China Horse' episode is the third 'flagpole' moment of this narrative. It happened when my brother Joseph was born, child number ten and the last of the 'tribe'. As usual we were scattered to the four winds as there must have been post-natal complications. I was sent to a family who lived down the street called the Fullers. They were a nice kind family who already had four children of their own and did not have anywhere for me to sleep. I was put in their lounge, the room no one went into unless they had visitors. I slept on a camp stretcher in this room and every night when I turned over it capsized and fell on top of me. Every night I picked myself up and went back to sleep. Mrs Fuller was the neatest, tidiest person it's possible to 'find in a day's march' as my father used to say. She dusted, polished, swept and wiped ceaselessly and everywhere all the surfaces gleamed and shone. Shoes were not allowed to be worn in the house. From their house I could nearly see my house but was on no account allowed to wander down the street to visit. This was strictly forbidden. And so there I was exiled and again abandoned, or that's how it felt. As time went on and it did, I wondered if I would ever see my mother again or return home. How long I was there I do not know but it felt like at least two months. I know that by the time I saw my latest new-born sibling he did not look at all like a new-born and the memory of my first glimpse of him is quite strong. As my homesickness mounted and my wondering about my mother got more intense I started standing outside the Fuller's gate after school in my school uniform and staring down the street to our house awaiting and hoping for deliverance or at least a glimpse of someone coming my way.

One day I was rewarded as I saw my father peddling in my direction. He was doubling a child on the bar of his bike. My heart missed a beat as they progressed in my direction. Suddenly Mary Fuller appeared at my side, clearly flustered. 'Susie', she said 'come away from the gate and come with me I have something amazing to show you'. I felt torn but always obedient and I reluctantly followed her inside the front door of their house. She stopped just inside the door, pointed to a highly polished table on which a china horse stood standing on its hind quarters and said 'look at this china horse'. This china horse had always been there along with copious renditions of similar objects as Mary was very keen on horses. I looked up at her in a puzzled way and then realised that I had been completely tricked. Someone had phoned from our house and instructed them to remove me from my watching post on the footpath. This task fell to Mary, who was about seventeen at the time. She was not gifted with a fertile imagination and her lame attempt at luring me away for reengagement away from the gate had failed completely. This was the earliest moment in my life when the first inklings of a realisation trickled through my consciousness that adults were flawed. I looked up at her with a questioning look as to how she could possibly think that this china horse would distract me from my true purpose of pleading my cause with the approaching cyclist to return home. Even something delicious to eat or a chocolate might have distracted me momentarily but I was not duped by this ridiculous horse and she knew it. Hithertofore, I had an impatience to become an adult, as I would no longer commit sins and not risk flames of some sort. After this occurrence I started to question this and the first seeds of doubt were sown about the "goodness" of adults.

Poor Mary, I do not blame her at all. She was a pawn in an act of trickery and she knew that too. I must reiterate that the Fullers were good kind people. Mr Fuller was aware of my unhappiness and often tried to cheer me up. Mrs Fuller was brisk and efficient and the teenage Fuller boys were kind to me. Much later after they moved from this house much further away. I would visit them often and one incident stands out which needs to be related. I had ridden my bike after school to their house. It was a beautiful fine day and I was frolicking out on their back lawn with one of their sons called Bernard. He was an amiable teenager of sixteen and he was kind to me both when I was exiled at their place a few years earlier and subsequently. We were rolling around having play fights when Mrs Fuller called out 'Susie would you like to stay for tea. We are having sausages'. I stopped in my tracks as, at that very moment I happened to accidently touch a part of Bernard's anatomy which I shouldn't have. I stared in disbelief at Bernard and replied 'Mrs Fuller I think Bernard has them down his pants!' The look of horror which passed over Bernard's face still remains with me. I knew immediately that I had uttered something truly dreadful but in that split second I actually did believe that Bernard did have some sausages down his pants. I had four brothers but had only seen that part of the anatomy in flaccid form and had no idea that it could change to such an extent. I knew then, as I did when I asked Mrs Hills if she read books, that it was time to peddle swiftly home and so I did.

I have no recollection if I ever went back to Fullers again as I puzzled long and hard over this incident. It is since become an often told story in our family but I have always worried about the effect on Bernard of this incident. He was a lovely sensitive boy who was kind enough to play with a nine-year-old and he did not deserve this humiliation. Equally, there was no intention on my part to make him feel bad in any way as I was as innocent as the day is long. From that day to this I have never looked at a sausage impartially and I wonder if he has either.

Chapter 7 – My Parents

A Digression from the School and Education Narrative

Dear Amelia and Fionn:

I am going to digress for a while to explain my progenitors and where they came from as far as I am able. I feel it is appropriate to sketch in for you as far as my perception and scant knowledge allows some background information.

My mother was born Isabel Cecily O'Regan the youngest of six children. Her brother Teddy had died of the Spanish flu in 1917 and one can only surmise that this was a traumatic event for her at the age of nine. She had one other sister Clare who became a sister of Mercy and whose brand of religion was as extreme as my mother's became. On her visits to see us in Palmerston North she made it her mission to corner one of us, fix us with her piercing grey/blue beady penetrating eyes, and enquire with her soft menacing voice 'have you got a vocation?' She was very good at finding a spot from which there was no escape, such as behind the huge living room table from which egress necessitated clambering over it and she had a soft breathy quiet purring voice. The right side of her mouth went up to form a small aperture so that the words whistled as they were funnelled out of that side of her mouth. 'I think so' I would answer breathlessly. 'Speak to me about it when you are sure'. As if any of us would go anywhere near her should we hear the clarion call to become a Bride of Christ.

Much later when I got contact lenses and made the mistake of telling her she turned on me with great alarm to warn me that these were terrible things and that I would definitely get eye cancer further down the track. By far the worst thing she ever did concerned my eldest sister MaryClare who on the eve of her marriage to Louis Morganti received a letter from Aunty Clare, as we called her, warning her of the momentous step she was taking in eschewing her true bridegroom Christ and entering the mirky terrain of a liaison with an earthly bridegroom. 'Think, ponder pray' she counselled. I never saw that letter, but those three words have become embedded in the lexicon of our family as a set phrase of warning when a dire step is about to embarked upon. Once when she was visiting my grandmother in Avon Street, she encountered my cousin Dorothy standing at the kitchen sink wearing shorts. She stood stock still at the kitchen door, turned in horror to the nun following her saying 'back sister, back sister'. This nun was called Sister Lawrence. She was an art teacher obsessed with the colour yellow ochre, so much so that she was actually called "Yellow Ochre" behind her back. She stopped with such haste that a minor collision occurred and she beat a hasty retreat. Aunty Clare expostulated with my cousin Dorothy as to the unacceptable levels of immodesty she was exhibiting. I guess that legs were not something she had encountered much at all in her life and the sight of them exposed was a great shock. Now 'back sister' is an accepted rejoinder to anyone in our family who is about to see something that should not be seen.

My mother had three brothers, Patrick, Rolland and Cornelius. The eldest Patrick had gone to live in Inangahua after he became ill with the 1917 flu and was advised by his doctor to seek a life on the land in the open air. Thus he abandoned his legal studies and did just that, fathering eight children while he was at it. When I was fifteen I ventured down to the Inangahua Junction with my friend Joan Walters and stayed with Uncle Pat and Aunty Helen. The latter was my god mother but she did not feature at all in my life and certainly paid no attention to my religious wellbeing, for which I was grateful. There were plenty of others attending to that.

Her brother Rolland was a surgeon and a man whose opinion of himself was not inconsiderable. We were all slightly in awe of him as he was surrounded by an aura of greatness because he was a doctor but more than that a surgeon. Such men occupied the pinnacle of the social hierarchy as their power lay in healing others and commanding a respect which sometimes lapsed into sycophancy on the part of others. He was married to Rena Bradshaw who was Ngai Tahu the principle Maori iwi of the south Island. Her son Tipene (who we called Steve and is now Sir Tipene) was one of the notable negotiators in the Ngai Tahu claims settlement in 1998. They had two other adopted children and lived for a long time in Hataitai Wellington. They had also taken into their home a woman called Rose O'Neill. Her role in their lives is unclear to me, but I know that she was sickly and my Uncle had found her during his medical activities. Later she married a man called Bernard Grant and they adopted a child whom they called Paddy. Bernard worked in Kirkcaldie and Stains, the large department in Wellington. He was a lift operator, and pressed the requisite buttons when a person got into the lift. Of course today it's 'do it yourself' in lifts but then, the operator was dressed in some finery and took the job very seriously. My aunt and uncle's house looked right over the sea and I recall staring transfixed at this beautiful view not knowing then how much the sea meant to me. Being brought up in an inland city and having scant access to the sea except places I was slightly afraid of, such as Himatangi Beach where we occasionally went. I did not know about this great love until I sought it out myself much later and now would find it hard to be away from.

I have spoken already about my mother's third brother Cornelius who we called Uncle Con. His life was marred by tragedy. He was the only member of my mother's family who appealed to me in any way as I saw and felt his benevolence. He used to take his neighbour Miss Evett who lived alone next door out for drives at the weekend. Sometimes he took me too if I was at my grandmother's place, which I often was. My cousin Mary often came on these jaunts and we would often sing in the back seat to while away whatever journey we were taking. Miss Evett would turn to us and in her rather posh voice say 'what beautiful voices you have' which we didn't really believe but they might have been when we were young and unselfconscious. All I could see of Miss Evett were the broken veins in her face, which I am ashamed to say made me feel rather repelled.

Religion played a big part in my mother's family but I cannot fathom why it gripped and obsessed the two women of the family in the extreme way it did. I could put forward some theories about the role and place of women in the first part of the 20th century which might go some way to explain it but I will refrain from that. My grandmother was a convert to the Catholic religion. Such people can sometimes become excessive in their zeal but I never observed this in my grandmother.

My mother had considerable musical talents. She was an excellent pianist and singer having her Licentiate of the Royal College of Music and the Royal Academy of Music in both piano and singing. She could also play the cello well. She had large hands and long fingers, which my sister Pauline, who is also musically talented, has inherited. My mother could play difficult piano pieces such as Liszt and Chopin both of which require great stretches of the fingers well past the octave. She later put this talent to good use by giving piano lessons not just to us but to some outside pupils as well. In Palmerston North she was part of a 'Musical Circle' who would go to each other's houses every month to sing and play the piano. I loved it when they came to our house and would lie in bed listening intently to the goings on in the 'front room' which is what we called the smart room in the house, where no one went except when we had visitors, especially nuns and priests. This would have made a much-needed extra bedroom as we were all squashed into the 'back room' where six of us slept. This was a sacrosanct space which had two couches and a smart armchair and the piano.

It also was the room where all the family photos were displayed and there were lots of them. All the weddings of my mother and father's brothers and sisters, pictures of their children on which I was 'tested' by the police after my abduction episode and passed with flying colours. There was the usual collection of framed holy pictures, such as The Sacred Heart, the Virgin Mary and Maria Goretti. Luckily Sister Collette's appalling statues didn't make the cut for this room. They were only good enough for the 'living room' or if unblessed useful for hopscotch as already mentioned. I was naturally a quietly nosy child whose antennae were always in full reception mode. I was listening and retaining everything and it is only now that I realise that this was what I was doing as I recall these details of my life. It kept me entertained for hours eavesdropping on adult conversations boring as they probably were. Once the Catholic Women's League of which my mother was an enthusiastic member put on a play. My mother had a small part. In fact she had one line 'Spots! What kind of spots?' I went to see it more than once and anxiously waited for my mother's one line almost bursting with pride as she uttered it.

Dear Amelia and Fionn: My Parents continued

And now to my father and what I know of him, which is not a great deal. Much of what I do know I have learned from my sister Pauline's excellent book entitled 'I Would Have Liked To Have Been A Nun' – the story of Isabel Cecily Dowling.

My father was born in Hokitika in 1904 the eldest of three boys of James and Mary (nee Warren) Dowling. In 1906 his father James a carrier, was buried alive in a gravel pit. My father was 3 years old and it is not too much to claim that this altered the course of his life quite significantly. There was no DPB in those days and his poor mother had to open a shop but in due course Mary married again. This time to a bridge builder called John O'Donnell. He already had one daughter, Maisie, and together they had another called Catherine (Cassie). The latter was to play a large part in my life some of which I have already related and more details of which will be recounted in due course. She often told us that he was a good, kind gentle brother who always brought her lovely presents from his overseas travels.

My father was not educated past primary school but eventually did an apprenticeship with Phoenix Iron and Brass Foundry, Robertson and Co Ltd, Engineers and Boiler. When this was complete he went to sea with the New Zealand Shipping Company and studied in London for his Chief Engineer's certificate. Going to London shows his courage and belief in himself. He had to do extra study in Mathematics in the evening in order to manage the work required for the certificate. He boarded in the East End and had a good kind landlady who liked my father. He would have been a tidy, considerate and thoughtful boarder so things worked out well. My father liked women probably more than men. He had seen first-hand the struggle his mother had had and being the eldest this had given him an awareness of a woman's lot. He would often recount the hardships of his mother with tears in his eyes. His emotions were close to the surface and he cried quite often. He would often be heard to say of women with feckless husbands who drank away the family income 'she's a saint that woman'. He was of course programmed according to the times as to what was expected of his daughters and their limited horizons but did have that extra awareness around the domestic expectations and during our childhood he often did the washing and brought it in off the line.

The washing was a herculean task both in the method and volume. In the early years it was done in a copper. This is a wash house boiler usually made of galvanised iron or in some cases copper. I do not remember what ours was made of. Imagine the volume when there would be at least two babies in napkins for many years. A fire was lit under the copper and it was filled with water. This was stirred at regular intervals with a long stick so the whole process was labour intensive. Eventually when it the washing had been boiled alive it was rinsed in a tub and put through a wringer which was of course worked by hand. The whole operation could take a good part of a day and that is why my father stepped in and helped with this time-consuming activity. After that it had to be hung on the lines which were stretched the length of our backyard and held up with a wooden prop. I can imagine that in winter this was hard to manage as the turnaround for the napkins needed to be as swift as possible. I often heard my father describe a wet baby as being 'as wet as a shag'. This might indicate that nappy-changing might have been delayed awaiting the drying of the washing. I never knew what he meant by this until years later and now I see shags on a daily basis ducking and diving and being constantly wet. It was a big day when we progressed to an Agitator washing machine which had a wringer which wrung without human intervention. This might be a false memory but I think some passing child accidently got an arm wrung in this device and there was much screaming until it was disabled. My father also bathed us. We did not welcome the bathing as he was vigorous and sometimes quite rough, but we certainly came out clean and well-rubbed.

I have talked about his considerable gardening skills already, but he also could do practical things outside the house and was a general handyman. He worked in Palmerston North for the Marine Department. This entailed travelling around doing annual inspections of lifts and boilers to make they were all safe for purpose. He sometimes had to travel out of town which we all looked forward to especially if you were chosen to sleep in my mother's bed. He had an office in the centre of town and a secretary called Miss Nugent. Sometimes in the school holidays one of us went to his office to help with some of the clerical work. I did this once but made of complete hash of what he had told me to do which was to glue down one edge of these square brown envelopes which probably contained information about all the venues he had to visit. I glued the wrong edge and he came home in a rage as Miss Nugent had to undo the damage. 'You useless article' he stormed while I cowered mainly in embarrassment at such a silly mistake. I'm sure that fear had interfered with my understanding of his instructions, but the term 'article' stuck and I later concluded that I was indefinite and incomplete as an article has to be attached to a noun to have any meaning and an indefinite article always refers to an unspecified thing. I have come across the word 'article' in Irish novels so my father had probably heard his Irish grandmother say it and had stored it up to use when an appropriate occasion arose.

He was a man who, if he had stopped having children after three, or even five, he would have remained good natured and lovable. My aunt Cassie, who was his half-sister, always told us that he was a generous, considerate brother who always brought great presents back when he came home from sea. She said he loved his mother and was an attentive son. However, because he was responsible, neat and tidy, the sheer numbers overwhelmed him. By the time I came along he was pretty much in a rage, so this is the father I encountered all my life. Someone I feared, who made me permanently anxious and whom I actually disliked. When I saw him lying in his coffin I felt nothing. I can now see how life's circumstances brought out the worst in him but fear kills feeling and so it did. He had a hard life in all respects. He genuinely loved my mother, and was affectionate towards her, which she mostly spurned, but for me he seemed to be a bomb awaiting the detonation of some event or pressure which occurred daily. He did not want ten children and who can blame him but he did have ten children and we all suffered as a consequence.

Even today I run a mile from angry men and have quite noticeably surrounded myself by non-aggressive men. Even hearing the roar of male voices at a rugby game sets up a reaction despite my efforts at rationalising the absurdity of it. I admired him greatly for the way he forged out a career, how he never drank or smoked and was a completely responsible father and husband. He had a terrible time during my mother's mental illness which began in earnest when I was 15 and which never went away with many dress rehearsals when babies were born in the form of probably undiagnosed post-natal depression. She ceased to be a mother, a wife and during the most intense time was scarcely a human being. This was horrible for him and he suffered greatly but so did we and our suffering was compounded by his reaction never allowing for what we were going through, thus delivering a double dose of helpless misery. This generation of fathers tended to experience their emotions without analysis. My father certainly did. Because of this they had trouble understanding their emotions and just felt them and usually projected them onto those nearby without a shred of cognisance as to the effect this would have. He could be witty and light-hearted but this was rare and when it occurred it was received with the awareness that it would probably be short-lived. He sometimes told us stories of life on board ship and we particularly liked the one where a tiger escaped and roamed around the ship while everyone hid and others tried to catch it. One man was leaning overboard and the tiger came along and bit him on the bottom. He would laugh uproariously at this and so would we but somehow we were also doubtful as to its veracity.

The picture is not complete without mentioning his inclination to use strange turns of phrase. Having been at sea he had developed the tendency to use nautical expressions such as 'square your yards' when he wanted one of us to disappear. 'Scutch to the bullsacks' was another utterance he made often and which to this day we do not know what it means. One definition of scutch as a noun means to be a real pain in the arse but the verb to scutch means to beat flax. Where the bull sacks (or perhaps he was saying ballsacks) came in remains a mystery. Whether it was something to do with bulls' testicles I will never know, but it probably was. He would accompany this verbal delight by vigorously flapping his right hand under his chin. This expression and the flapping movement has gone down in the family and been shared far and wide to cousins and even to friends. He also swore and blasphemed appallingly with expletives which were not common at the time but which became 'water off a duck's back' for us so often did we hear them. My mother too, became immune but would utter a hushing sound when he indulged in the more extreme examples, especially the blasphemous variety such as 'crucified Jesus' and 'merciless mongrels'. It is not drawing too long a bow to say this language was unusual in a devout catholic household but for us it was an everyday event. Once a month 'The Holy Name Society' had a special Sunday Mass which men would attend to renew vows to keep their language free from profane or contemptuous speech concerning God. My father attended these monthly masses and joined in the chorus at the end of Mass, proclaiming his intent to refrain from using the name of God in vain. From a young age I pondered on this confusing duality and wondered a lot.

Chapter 8 – Standard 4 and a flagpole moment

Dear Amelia and Fionn:

So we come to Standard 4. I am 10 years old. I leave the tranquil waters of Sister Elizabeth's class and sail into the shark infested waters of Sister Clothilde's class.

Sister Clothilde had been sent from Ireland to New Zealand as a Sister of Mercy at a young age. She was probably seventeen or eighteen. This was not uncommon. She would talk a lot of her childhood in Ireland with terrifying stories of what I can only describe as her father's cruelty. She did not describe it thus but would regale us with stories of his frequent beatings in response to some misdemeanour. 'My father would reach for the switch', she would say 'and he would sssssswitch us and sssssswitch us'. Her sibilance, already pronounced, doubled in strength and we would sit spell bound imagining the swish of the sssssswitch as it encountered young flesh. These accounts were a veiled salutary warning to us that there is also a sssswitch to hand in the classroom awaiting some transgression to warrant its use. This was a successful form of control and we would sit in dumb silence fearful that some action would justify the use of the switch. She did use it in the form of a leather belt, but such was my terror of this woman that nothing I did could ever justify the use of such a device on me. 'Woe betide' was one of her favourite expressions 'any person who talks while I am out of the room'. Only brave people would talk and I was not one of them. This archaic expression was used by lots of nuns and portended an outcome which one feared a great deal, especially when uttered by Sister Clothilde.

Sister Clothilde, who was called Chloe behind her back, had the cruellest face and the deadest eyes I have ever seen in a human being before or since. These eyes looked at one through rimless glasses. She would fix those dead eyes on you and you felt your soul wither within you. Your heart would set up a racket which caused your breath to come out in short desperate pants. I suppose anyone who had been subjected to some switch wielding bully all her young life would have had any finer feelings well and truly knocked out of her and would render her cold and

71

cruel but we were too young to make any allowances whatsoever. She preferred boys to girls and made this very plain. She taught us without humour or kindness and we absorbed her teachings in dumb fear. I recall the character of Squeers in Nicholas Nickleby by Charles Dickens. Squeers is the cruel and brutish headmaster of the school Nicholas attends where beatings are a daily occurrence. Eventually Nicholas bravely interferes during the savage beating of a boy who is a cripple and who has attempted to run away from the school. He grabs the stick and turns it on the headmaster then successfully escapes from the school with the boy.

The event which occurred and justifies being called 'a flagpole moment' happened in Standard 4. We were learning subject and predicate. This was a lesson which was supposed to teach us that every sentence contains two parts: a subject and a predicate. The subject is what (or whom) the sentence is about, while the predicate tells something about the subject. For example: The girl (subject) jumped over the fence (predicate). We had drawn two columns in our exercise books with one column labelled subject and the other labelled predicate. Sister Clothilde would call out a sentence and we would write it in the columns under the correct headings. We had done about 10 of these sentences and Sister Clothilde was wandering up and down the aisles looking at what we had done. I had dutifully headed up each page as we were expected to with the letters JMJ which of course stood for Jesus Mary and Joseph. At the foot of each page I had obediently written AMDG Ad Majorem Dei gloriam which meant 'For the greater glory of Christ', so I knew all was in order. She arrived at my desk and instructed me to go to the front of the class. Up went 'Goody Two Shoes' feeling smug and virtuous getting ready for the praise which would be heaped upon my head. And so it happened. Sister Clothilde looked at me, her two eyes looking like two dead filleted fish on a plate. There was no glint which I would have welcomed as it would have shown that there was some life there. She then began a litany of accolades drawing on my family for proof that I was an example to all to copy and emulate. 'Look at this clever girl standing in front of you. Her mother is a saintly woman' she said. 'She has an aunt a holy nun. Her grandfather is a judge. Her uncle is a renowned surgeon. Her other uncles are well known in the legal profession and are good, holy and just men. She comes from a large wonderful family so many children sent by God to populate his Holy Church'.

By this time I was puffed up with pride and bursting with confidence thinking how amazing I was and how lucky to come from such high quality stock. Then Sister Clothilde lowered her voice to a whisper, paused for what seemed like a lifetime, fixed the dead fish upon me and hissed 'And she can't even do subject and predicate. Now go back to your desk and correct your work'. I can hardly describe how I felt. I burst into tears, sobbing and shaking my way back to my desk oblivious to the sympathetic glances of my classmates. My legs had gone wobbly and would hardly carry me. My face was hot and I sat there numb unable even to pick up my pencil. I had no idea what I had done wrong, so was unable to correct my error. I had put subject 'The girl jumped' Predicate 'over the fence'. To be built up so definitively only to be brought crashing down in front of my classmates was a humiliation almost too much to bear. I wish I had been as brave as Nicholas Nickleby and turned the sssswitch on this cruel woman.

How much self-hatred must this woman be carrying that she could do this to an innocent ten-year-old and call it teaching. I was well behaved, quiet obedient and meek and too scared to be otherwise yet she fished me out from the classroom, dangled me on her sadistic line then reeled me in to annihilate me. This story has never left me. I have recounted it to various members in my family on many occasions. My sister Mary Clare was so horrified that she wrote a short story called 'Subject and Predicate'. I cannot recall whether I told my mother. I think by this time it felt pointless as my mother would listen abstractedly channelling Mrs Jellaby and make some fatuous rejoinder such as 'The nuns are holy women and they should be respected'. Much later I heard that Sister Clothilde had died at sea while travelling back to Ireland. She was cast into the eternal depths of the waves where live fish devoured those dead fishy eyes. At least eventually she provided sustenance to some living creatures.

During this year I also became a 'pioneer'. This had nothing to do with being an early settler but was a pledge taken to eshew alcoholic drink until my 21st birthday. This movement had its roots in Ireland of course and was founded by an Irish Jesuit. We would chant a recitation to this end which went like this:

For your greater glory and consolation

O Sacred Heart of Jesus and for your sake to give good example, to practice self denial.

To make reparation to you for the sins of intemperance

and for the conversion of excessive drinkers

I will abstain from all intoxicating drinks until my 21st birthday'.

Of course this meant nothing to me and, as already related, alcohol played no part in our lives but I robotically chanted the above and wore a special pin to add to all the other paraphernalia draped around my person.

Somehow I escaped the clutches of Sister Clothilde and progressed to Standard 5 and 6 and to the kind care of Sister Martina. The next two years passed peacefully and the trauma of Standard 4 faded. I did well during this time, always getting top in Catechism and always near the top of the class in other subjects. The word dunce was never applied to me, but it was used for other people sometimes. Earlier in the century, dull-witted children were made to sit in a corner with a Dunce's hat on, but this horrible and demeaning practice had disappeared at the time I was being educated.

I played basketball constantly, high jumped incessantly and played ball games with Joan Walters at every opportunity. I was young for my age physically and mentally and, although I was twelve, I looked more like a nine-year-old. I was and always will be a 'late developer' physically, mentally and emotionally. During this time Sister Martina, in her wisdom decided to show the 'mature' girls a film about their emerging womanhood. She selected those she thought were ready and I was not one of them. She was right and even five years later I was not ready.

The girls she chose were already 'developed' as was said of early maturity. Girls such as Adriana Dematina and Rosalie McDowell who were extremely 'developed'. They, and another couple of girls, were in a group of their own and if they have to be labelled let me call them 'outsiders'. Adriana was a large Maori girl and Rosalie was tall with a great amount of acne. She was so shy and unhappy that if you spoke to her she would blush and often cry. She kept her eyes lowered at all times. I do not know the genesis of her unhappiness but the word was that her parents were old and she was an only child, two afflictions which were used to explain this poor girl's vulnerability. In the 1950's being a tall girl was completely undesirable. They were always in the back row of school photos and always stooped in an effort to look shorter. The era of the tall fashion plate had not yet arrived.

.Just before I went to board at St. Mary's my mother tried in a very clumsy way to inform me of things to come by telling me that the time would come when I would lose a 'drop of blood' and that was fine and normal and to be expected so when the Huka Falls arrived I was terrified and thought that I was about to die. My mother handed me some rags and some safety pins to deal with this and left me to it. The rags were discarded kitchen roller towels and smelt of onions as many an oniony hand had been wiped on them. I was not sure what to do with the pins but somehow I managed but the overriding feeling was one of shame and a desperate need to not let anyone know or see. My sisters were of course going through the same thing but there was no information sharing as they too felt the same as I did. We used to sneak around try to put discarded unmentionable things in the chip heater in the kitchen when my father wasn't looking but that was not easy as he was always on the lookout for any interference in matters of his domain. What we did in Summer when there was no chip heater has been erased from my memory.

Chapter 9 – Friends and Friendship

Dear Amelia and Fionn:

I am now leaving the narrative about my education and school years to tell you about my friends. It is an appropriate time as I leave primary school and go up to Form 3 at St Joseph's High School in Palmerston North.

My first friend was Helen Morpeth and I met her when I was three years old as our mothers were friends. Our friendship lasted right through school and spasmodically after that. Helen was fearless in equal proportion to my being fearful. Throughout our childhood we would go on adventures led by her. She would do incredibly daring things while I bleated on the sideline watching her climb and clamber in what I considered to be risky situations. She literally had no fear and in the end she perished at the age of forty doing something risky. My knowledge of the detail is sketchy, but I know that she fell through ice and drowned in Denmark while walking out to take a photo. I believe that she had a boyfriend in Norway and was there for that reason. Once when we were much older she persuaded me not to wear a hat in church. Now to the modern reader this does not sound like a rebellious act but in the context of the time it was. It was about covering our hair and we can all blame St Paul who thought that women's hair was a source of temptation to men.

'God's word is that women should submit to their husbands and that wearing a veil is intended to demonstrate that submission'. I decided for once to be brave and go along with Helen's suggestion so hatless into the church we went. We paid dearly for this. The priest who was a dour joyless example of humanity called Father Fowler. He decided to make us the subject of his sermon while staring at us for the duration of his instructive talk. He mentioned St Paul often and his beady mean eyes bore down on us. I was completely intimidated as the shackles of Catholic conformity were still firmly attached to all parts of my mind and body. Helen stared brazenly back at him. He was probably consigning her to the darkest recesses of hell while he probably saw in my cringing figure some hope of redemption.

Helen lived at first on the edge of the boundary of Palmerston North in Tremain Avenue. In fact she lived near where my abductor tried to drag me over the barbwire fence almost opposite Helen's house. Later her family moved to Carlton Avenue. She always had dogs. They were always small and yappy and I was always terrified of them as they barked and jumped and ran up to me in a manner which I construed as menacing. There was one dog in particular called Jerry who did all these things while Helen said repeatedly 'He won't hurt you.' I was never convinced as all dog owners utter this mantra no matter what behaviour their beloved beast is manifesting. At this stage I need to clarify my position on dogs. I like dogs but I am cautious around them until I know them. I think they are the most amazing animals whose loyalty and intelligence cannot be questioned, but if an unknown dog runs up to me barking I am terrified. If snarling is added to that mix then I could faint with fear. When their devoted owners pronounce that they just want to befriend me, which owners invariably do, I want to render damage to their person.

Helen's parents were unusual. Her father was not a Catholic and was much older than her mother. Although his name was Gerald, he was called Tad. We were told that his parents thought he looked like a tadpole when he was born so Tad it was. He was a quiet but kind man who read a lot and their house had a lot of books in it. He died when Helen was twelve years old and was the first parent of my contemporaries to die. He ran a bottle recycling business, although it was not called that in the 1950's, and had a large warehouse in Rangitikei Street where Helen and I would venture after school. The bottle crates were stacked from ground to ceiling and up Helen would clamber without hesitation. I would stand at the bottom begging her not to go higher, but up she went regardless. I did not even venture to the first level as the crates were not secured, simply piled on top of one another and in my mind ready to crash to the ground at any point. They always wobbled precariously as Helen went higher and higher. However, she never came to any harm. She did however, come to harm when she was climbing some agricultural device which was sitting in the field opposite her house. This machine was round and had thick protuberances which was probably used at to break up dry stubborn soil. Up Helen clambered with the usual musical accompaniment of my cries. As she neared the top, the machine began to roll and one of the thick knobs went straight into her lower leg. She howled with pain and fell to the ground. Her mother was not far away and came hurtling over to the field. She cast an accusing eye at me, but quickly realised that I was innocent and would not have encouraged this folly and knew Helen would not have responded to any calls to desist even if they had been uttered. I scuttled home while Helen was rushed to hospital. She recovered in due course but always had an impressive scar to show for this misadventure.

Helen's mother was kind to me. She was always dressed in tweeds with paisley scarves and always wore a felt hat to church. She drove a Humber car with leather seats and had a loud posh voice. The volume went up when she was summoning Helen, but it was never in anger but often in exasperation. I was always welcome and often stayed overnight at their house. Because Helen was unusual she did not have many friends. Sometimes at school I was torn as other friends claimed my attention but I tried to stay loyal to her despite the pull of the more popular factions. Helen was original, creative and intelligent. She was also very good at sport especially high jumping and no one could jump as high as she could. She wrote poems and plays and insisted that I play the central role in her creations. I was happy to oblige. When we were age fourteen she wrote a play called Mr Arlington. It was a murder mystery and we performed it far and wide. I played the main role of Mr Arlington and had great fun doing it. She cast all classmates in the other roles, regardless of talent. One of these talentless participants had one line only. She had to say the words 'Twelve O'clock' as she raised her wrist and looked at her watch. No amount of training could get her to coordinate these actions. 'Twelve O'clock' she would say, then raise her wrist to look at her watch. In the end we gave up and allowed the comic element to prevail. This girl was hugely intelligent at schoolwork but dramatic timing was impossible for her to grasp.

My other friend from the beginning of school until I left to board at St. Mary's in Wellington was Joan Walters. Joan was a shy child and probably was shy most of her life. She had blond curls, blue eyes a small nose and a peaches and cream complexion, not a freckle in sight These looks were exactly what the 1950's saw as textbook and countless popular film stars such as Debbie Reynolds and Doris Day had these facial qualities. I had straight brown hair, a nose heading towards aquiline and from the age of nine I wore glasses. But worst of all I was covered in freckles. How I hated those freckles. So much so that when I spied an advertisement in the *Tablet* for a product called *Kintho* which promised to 'clear ugly freckles away from the skin in just a few short days', it got my attention. I waited until this issue of the *Tablet* held no more interest for anyone. I surreptitiously cut out the advertisement, snuck to the Post Office for a postal note of the right amount and sent off for this miracle cure. Then I waited nervously for it to arrive, hoping that I would be at the letterbox to grab it before anyone else saw it and thus circumvent any ridicule from the perch dwellers which might come my way. As luck would have it I got to it first and eagerly started to apply it. After a few days I did notice some fading but I also felt my skin go dry and scaly as of course this 'miracle' cure had bleach in it, in fact was probably all bleach. Such was my discomfit that I stopped using it after about a week and quickly the faded freckles resumed their usual vibrancy.

Joan Walters was an easy friend who never sulked or said mean things. She came from a family of six children and the best thing was that her mother was Brown Owl. So of course I joined the Brownies as soon as I could. Her father sold second-hand cars so they always had nice cars such as Rovers. He was a quiet man as were many of my friends' fathers it seems. I never heard Mr Walters utter a single word. He defined taciturnity. Perhaps I noticed because I had such a noisy father. Mrs Walters was a kind warm person and as Brown Owl she presided over a happy pack of Brownies. We met every Saturday and stood around the toadstool and declared 'to promise to do my best, to do my duty to God and the Queen, to help other people every day especially those at Home'. Our motto was to 'lend a hand' Pretty quickly I was made a 'sixer' which meant I was head of my patrol of six brownies and worked hard to get as many badges on the arms of my uniform as possible. There was a variety of these such as cooking, sewing, swimming, gardening and other domestic skills. I joined at the age of 8 and flew up to Guides when I was 11. Flying up was a ceremony of some significance and one literally did fly as Brown Owl and Tawny Owl held you aloft as you jumped over the toadstooll, never to return.

While I was a Brownie I went on holiday with the Walters family to Taupo. Looking back I often wonder at families adding other children to their load, when they have plenty of their own to cater for, but in this case the two oldest girls Elaine and Anne did not come as they were old enough to stay home alone so there were five children and two adults. We travelled with a laden trailer and a roof rack stacked high. We camped at Kinloch at the camping ground right next to the lake. We stayed three weeks, during which time Mr Walters disappeared back to Palmerston North most of the time it seems, probably to attend to his second-hand car business. We all slept in the same tent and cooked outside on the barbeques supplied. Next to our tent was a family who were great fun. They called me 'Sue Bun' as they had a Chinese greengrocer by that name. They gave me the chance to learn to water ski which I tried a few times but was an abject failure, so they gave up. The strong memory of this holiday was the terrible coldsores I developed on my lips. The sun was relentless and protection was minimal at that time. These coldsores were terribly painful that I found it hard to eat. My lips were literally crusted both upper and lower. Apart from that it was a good holiday and Mrs Walters always made me feel welcome. However, those coldsores did blight my time by the lake at Kinloch.

So, Amelia and Fionn: at the age of ten I flew up to Guides, leaving Brown Owl, Tawny Owl and the toadstool behind.

Here we pronounced 'on my honour I promise that I will do my best, to do my duty to God and the Queen, to help other people at all times and to obey the Guide law'. Again our motto was 'be prepared'. Our Captain who we called Cap was a person called Marie Hay. Her family owned a hardware shop in Rangitikei Street called Hay and Watson which was the only such shop in Palmerston North at the time so was a thriving business. Marie Hay smoked incessantly which seemed perfectly natural in these days when smoking was accepted as normal. She had developed a brown discolouration around the edges of her nose from smoke exhalation. They had a house in Elmira Avenue and as I progressed up the Guiding hierarchy I often went there to discuss things. I used to stare in awe at that house. It had luxuriant wall to wall carpet, venetian blinds and large chintzy comfortable armchairs the like of which I had never seen before. There were china ornaments on every spare surface which looked expensive as well as opulent looking lamps on highly polished tables. The kitchen had a stainless-steel bench and to my young eyes it was pure luxury compared to our house where my father pronounced regularly 'sacks and bags are good enough for kids!' There were two other children in 'Cap's' family one of whom was called Beryl and who was handicapped in some way and was ushered from the room if she poked her head in. The other was a rather rotund indulged looking son who no doubt followed his father's footsteps into the family business. I loved going to that house to wallow in the tidiness and to my eyes, opulence of it. We were always given light refreshments and these were always delicate and delicious.

During my time in the Guides we went on many camps and learned to pitch tents, cook on an open fire, make shoe racks for our shoes out of tree branches and make damper. We also gazed up into the dark sky and learned about the Southern Cross and the night sky. I liked these camps and had a lot of fun at them. The leaders were always kind and one or two were actually overgrown school girls as I think guiding holds some allure for such people. One kept repeating the mantra 'While there's life there's hope' for some reason. She was a stout jolly person who liked a bit of fun so fun we had.

I acquired every badge possible and soon both sleeves of my guide uniform was studded with these achievements. Eventually I acquired the highest award called the All-Round Cord. To get this one had to pass a large number of tests and achievements and acquire efficiency badges. As well as this one had to be a leader, as well as loyal to God and the Queen. This cord was looped around the shoulder and under the arms and worn at the top of the sleeve and held in by a buttoned flap. So now I was trussed up by two cords as the pink and white plaited Philomena cord was always tucked away out of sight around my waist protecting me from the perils of Palmerston North's underbelly, and external whenever I wore my Guide uniform when the All-round Cord was on display.

The absolute acme of Guiding was the Queen's Guide award. I think its equivalent today is the Duke of Edinburgh award. I began working towards this but left before I had got very far to board at St Mary's in Wellington. Did I question this movement? No I did not. When you come from a large family who for many years did not have a car one looks for distraction and entertainment elsewhere. It was a great way to see my friends at weekends. There were no beaches nearby. Everything we did had to be within biking distance.

Another one of my friends right from the age of five until I left for St. Mary's was Aileen Shaw. She was slightly on the periphery as she had a best friend called Judy Pine with whom she hung out all the time. I was slotted in from time to time especially as she lived quite close to me in Matipo Street near the boundary of the city. Aileen's father was dead leaving Mrs. Shaw with eight children. Aileen was the youngest. There was no DPB in those days so Mrs Shaw had to work and did so in a fish and chip shop in the Main Street. Mrs Shaw was a most amazing woman. So many times I saw her peddling to work around 5 o'clock in the afternoon hail, rain or shine. She was always cheerful and calm despite her struggle. Their house bespoke poverty but the occupants did not at all reflect that reality. The Shaw family was cheerful and resilient and all grew up to be great citizens and achievers. Once I had occasion to open a cupboard in their kitchen and was shocked to see how bare it was. Their furniture was sparse and their house was in a state of disrepair.

Her first two children were boys and as they grew they became a great support to Mrs Shaw. Two of her daughters Angela and Gabrielle became nuns but they did not stay the course. Angela Shaw was my sister Philippa's best friend and she was a sensitive soul who always had the grace to speak to me kindly. She came to our house often. When I was struck down with Trench mouth I had to be isolated in our sunporch for three weeks. This horrible gum disease is painful. One's mouth is filled with ulcers which bleed at the slightest provocation. I had to rinse my mouth out with salt water twice a day which hurt a lot. I was not allowed out and had to eat bland food and copious liquids. I was very bored and isolated but I have a strong memory of how kind Angela Shaw was during this time. She would stand outside my window and talk to me for a long time. This made a huge impression on me and I would look forward to her visits. Her sister Aileen was a confident child, perhaps being the youngest of eight she got extra attention from those above her.

Once a week our class went to the Technical College to have sewing and cooking lessons and Aileen and I would often hang out after these classes. Usually we made a beeline for the bridge nearby which spanned the road and tipped our cooking straight into the stream below. These classes were very tedious. The cooking teacher was called Miss Cotton and the sewing teacher was called Miss Cook. This strange juxtaposition of their names was not lost on us. Miss Cotton invariably had very long manicured nails and we would watch with intense fascination as she dipped them in a dough mixture with the instruction 'knead the dough girls...like so'. As she did this we watched in utter fascination as a large part of the dough edged itself under these shaped claws. She would proceed to pick the dough out and return it to the bowl. Little wonder that the eels in the stream under the bridge on the way home were the recipients of our culinary efforts. Miss Cook the sewing teacher did not inspire me at all. I am not naturally drawn to sewing so these lessons bored me a great deal and the fruits of my labours were usually dismal failures. I once made a cotton petticoat which was so misshapen and large that my entire family could have snuggled down inside it. I did, however, make a child's smocked dress which was a success and was put to good use somewhere.

Because the mass production of clothes had not taken hold particularly in women's fashion, NZ women were expected to be adroit with the needle, both large for knitting and small for sewing. I was not naturally inclined in this way but all my sisters were. However, I thought it behoved me to do this given my gender so without examination of this expectation I ploughed on producing garments which were usually not successful. I never seemed to master the art of 'cutting out' using wafer thin patterns. Cutting out the garment is a key ingredient to a good outcome but despite my best efforts I could not form an attachment to this activity. Fortunately my mother had a friend called Mrs Lavin who was a consummate seamstress and so neat that one stared in awe at her output. She had a husband called Jack who with my father was a member of the Third Order of St Francis. This involved dressing up in brown Franciscan Friar robes and gathering at Mass thus dressed. I think Jack liked doing this but I think my father may have done these things under duress. When one went for a fitting to the Lavin's, Jack always seemed to be hanging over a steaming bowl with a towel over his head at the kitchen table. I wondered hard and long at this strange ritual but eventually worked it out that he was inhaling an infusion in order to clear his head cold which he always seemed to have. No one did that in our family.

At some point in our history the Franciscan Order set up a house in Fitzherbert Avenue. As my father was a member of the Third Order of St Francis , coupled with my mother's ability to sniff out any new shoot or branch with a Catholic odour which burst into life in Palmerston North, it was not long before these Friars became regular visitors to our house. The two who came the most were Father Simon Peter, a very good-looking young man and Brother Andrew. The hallmark of the latter was his tendency to utter the phrase 'ssssssss stuff and nonsense Mrs Dowling, ssssss stuff and nonsense' whenever he was slightly amused by something. We would sit with our antennae on the ready in eager anticipation of this utterance and derived a great deal of amusement from it so much so that to this day in some quarters of the family this strange habit continues to have currency. My father also befriended the Abbot at a Capuchin Monastery in Inglewood. 'I saw my friend the Abbot today' he would proudly declare. Perhaps he inspected their boiler but he considered the Abbot a personal friend and would call on him often. Maybe he liked the air of peace, quiet and order at the monastery and perhaps he even pondered on his choices as he re-entered his world of comparative disorder.

Because of friendship with the Franciscans we formed a connection with some Catholic Columbo Plan students who were studying at Massey University. Sometimes these students from Malaysia came for dinner at our house. It is no recorded as to their opinion of our food but I can imagine how bland they found it. It was decided that they should come to our house and cook one of their meals. We had not reckoned on the chillis. Here the clash of cultures was starkly revealed which even the shared membership of the Catholic church could not neutralise and we all sat gasping and gulping water as we munched our way through what today I would have appreciated as absolutely delicious. It was the first time I had ever had rice served with the main dish and not as a pudding.

My mother gave music lessons to the Lavin children in return for her doing sewing for us. Mrs Lavin had one failing and that was she tended to make everything too big allowing for growth so often her finished products did not fit and hung somewhat loosely. She had a daughter called Helen who was a year older than I was. Helen was somewhat rotund and I was long and skinny. However, without fail Helen's clothes were handed on to me and without fail 'hung' on me. When I was young I neither noticed nor minded but as I got older I became aware of looking like a sack of potatoes and began to resist a bit.

Other friends were on the periphery of my life were Diane Ongley, Judy Pine and Lesley Hogg. They drifted in and out of my activities but were never the main thing. Diane Ongley could draw well and despite zero encouragement in this area of our lives she clearly had talent. The only 'creative' thing we ever did was gothic lettering and to this day I have absolutely no skill whatsoever at drawing as you will know – Amelia and Fionn – from my sad attempts when we are playing Pictionary. Judy Pine's father coached basketball at both the schools and gave an enormous amount of his time voluntarily doing this. I recall one incident involving Mr Pine which occurred after a Saturday morning basketball event at the local intermediate school. Someone had to take the basketball back to school and Helen Morpeth and I were trying not to be the one to do it so we were throwing it back and forth to one another. To escape her I ran into the toilets and in my haste I did not notice that I had run into the men's toilets and as luck would have it Mr Pine was in there fully exposed urinating. I stared in horror and he did too before he found his voice and yelled 'hey, hey hey'. I will never forget those three heys and I ran for my life and it was some time before I could act normally in front of Mr Pine. Lesley Hogg's father was the city engineer and they lived in a big and to me opulent house with lush carpet everywhere and a wide sweeping staircase leading mysteriously upstairs. What puzzled me then was why did most of the parents of my friends never darken the door of the church? Only Mrs Morpeth seemed to, but I never saw the rest.

I have said many times that I was meek and timid and that is largely true, especially in my encounters with authority figures. However, there were times when I was with a group of friends that I became quite bold. This was group courage I suppose. On one such occasion we were wandering around and got hungry so decided to go to the fish and chip shop in Main Street and order fish and chips to feed us all. The plan was that when it came to pay, we would turn fruitlessly to one another saying 'You've got the money, haven't you?' In the end no one had the money and never did. The exasperated shopkeeper knew that he could not do anything with the fish and chips so shuffled us out of the shop where we gleefully ate the fish and chips. This dishonest act gnawed on my conscience and I contemplated this breach of the fifth commandment 'Thou shalt not steal' with great fear and trembling as I knew hell fire awaited me should I 'pass' unexpectedly. I bore this for two weeks, saved two-shillings, which was the cost of these ill-gotten gains, and biked to the shop on the way home from school. Then I ran into the shop and slapped the two-shillings on the counter and ran out. The astonished shopkeeper watched my departing figure in surprise and I sped away on my bike with my conscience washed clean.

Another group mischief was to walk around Featherstone Street, knock on a door and ask if we could have a drink of water. Most people looked at our supposedly innocent faces and invited us in and provided us with a glass of water which we drank and left. Once however, Lesley Hogg giggled so much that she wet the floor. Quickly we slid a chair over the offending patch and beat a hasty retreat. I probably told this in confession and am not sure how I phrased it as this sin had no precedent and therefore no handy vocabulary to describe it. Maybe I said 'I took advantage of my neighbour's kindness' and hoped that the priest did not ask for further details. Sometimes I visited my friend Maureen O'Meeghan who lived in College Street. I would go there with Helen Morpeth as Maureen and Helen were good friends. Her parents both smoked so there was ready access to cigarettes and matches lying around. We stole a packet and crept down to the bank of a stream which was at the bottom of their section. There we lit up. It was such a horrible experience of coughing and spluttering that I never repeated it.

I have noticed in my life that loners often befriend and seek me out. One of these loners was Maria Noara. She had Italian parents and lived with her mother and brother called Luigi who was, at least when I was around, quiet and uncommunicative. Her father had been killed in a level crossing accident a few years earlier. Life was not easy for Mrs Noara. She had to work hard in her job as well as bring up these two children and keep her house and garden. I think she was always sad which is to be expected as she would not have expected to be a widow at such a young age. She has a soft nature and found it difficult to exert her authority over

86

her young and strong-willed children. She had quite a pronounced lisp and when she said my name her tongue came slightly out the left side of her mouth so my name sounded like 'Sthusie'. I really liked Maria Noara. She was large, warm and generous and I spent a lot of time at their place and often stayed overnight. Again I gazed in awe at the interior of this house with its plush carpets, Venetian blinds and Formica benchtop with not a single thing on it. We had a wooden bench in our kitchen which as it aged got quite slimy despite frequent scrubbing. It always seemed to be cluttered. Pictures adorned the walls of Maria's house, some with cut glass mirror frames. There was one of the Virgin Mary at which I stared so hard that Mrs Noara took it off the wall and gave it to me. I was absolutely speechless with amazement and treasured this picture for years. It was at their house that I tasted spaghetti which was not out of a tin. I loved it. Later Maria Noara became the president of the New Zealand Elvis Presley fan club.

There were other 'loners' who attached themselves to me. One was Maud Barnes who came to our school in Standard 5 and had no friends. Maud was the neatest person one could imagine. She had lovely olive skin, not a freckle in sight and absolutely straight shiny brown hair. Her uniform was always neat as a pin and she was a quiet person. We struck up a bond and I would often go to her house and stay. They lived on a farm in the country. She too had an extremely quiet father and brother who from what I could see never uttered a word. Maybe they had no idea what to say to me, but her mother was chatty and kind.

Another loner was Teresa Crowe who attached herself to me and Joan Walters. Teresa lived out at Tokomaru and had done her primary schooling at the local school out there as her father was the headmaster. She arrived at St Joseph's in the 3rd form. Teresa was a shy person and very unsure of herself. She was terribly good and everything she said was uttered in a rather stilted manner as though she was apologising for speaking. Joan and I reluctantly allowed her to penetrate our inner sanctum. She used to talk about swimming at Darkies, which was a swimming hole near where they lived. I did experience this beautiful spot and wonder if today it is able to be swum in, reflecting that if not it is a terrible indictment on intensive farming practices which have been adopted in this area of the Manawatu.

Teresa trained as a nurse and at the conclusion of her training decided to enter the contemplative life of the Carmelite nun. This was an unsurprising choice for her. I visited her at the Carmelite Convent in Christchurch a few years later and waited patiently while locks were unlocked, sliding doors pushed back. I was led into a small room with a grill and a curtain preventing me from seeing Teresa but I was able to speak with her for fifteen minutes. This visit made an impression on me as there was an aura of peace and tranquillity which was apparent and I was fascinated by the simplicity of their lives and part of me could not let go of the abhorrence of the limitation that these nuns had imposed on their lives firm in the belief that God exists and every moment of their lives was devoted to his service.

When I was in London in the late 60's Teresa used to write to me quite often. I'm not sure that I wrote back but one memorable occasion I had taken her letter to read on the Tube. The Tube was crowded, with standing room only. I ripped open her letter and out on the tube floor fell a pile of holy pictures of various sorts including The Virgin Mary, The Sacred Heart and one of St Teresa. I was mortified and hastily retrieved them hoping no one had noticed. Here I was in swinging London dressed in my hotpants, high boots with my Mary Quant haircut so saccharine holy pictures, nay bad art were not part of my image. I imagine Teresa is still a Carmelite nun and if so she has been one for over fifty years.

And so I turn to another friendship which was an important one and much more one of equals. Susan Cowan came with her family to live in Palmerston North from Gisborne when I had just started secondary school and was thirteen years old. Her father had been appointed Headmaster of Central Normal school which was directly opposite our house. Unusually, Mrs Cowan was not a Catholic. There were four children in the family. Barbara who was a nun. Paul who was an accountant in Palmerston North, Susan and Johnny. Susan and I had many interests in common. We both played the piano, she much better than me. She was academically clever and shot to the head of the class without delay. We both liked to sing and she played tennis. I discovered tennis when I moved over to St Joseph's High School when I was thirteen. There was a tennis court at the school and as already mentioned one across the road at Central Normal School which we were allowed to use. Once I picked up a tennis racket I have seldom put it down except during my London days. In our house no one owned a racket. We simply took what was free at the time. Susan had a great sense of humour and we laughed a lot. Even better she lived around the corner from me in Annandale Avenue so we spent a lot of time together.

Sometimes I played tennis with Bogdan Kominowski. He became the famous pop star Mr Lee Grant. I did know until much later that he had actually been born in a Nazi concentration camp outside Dusseldorf and he and his mother emigrated to New Zealand. His father had died in the camp. I knew that he was Polish but that is where my curiosity at that stage of my life dried up. He was good-looking and good at tennis and he was also a nice person with a sad past which none of us knew anything about.

And now the sad part. Her brother Johnny was a beautiful child. He had soft brown eyes and a beautiful angelic face but at the age of four years old he slowed down developmentally and never advanced. This was a most terrible blow to the family. Suddenly this much-loved boy became a burden upon the family which had huge repercussions for the rest of their lives. It was discovered that he had inherited a gene from the maternal side which no one had known about until it manifested itself in Johnny. For the parents it was challenging. Mr Cowan was quite a stern man but with a quiet warmth and, although I could have been a bit in awe of him I wasn't, because I was always greeted fulsomely into that family and welcomed without restraint. Mrs Cowan had a quiet dignity and always received me with enthusiasm. Johnny would run up to me and fling his arms around me shouting 'Sue Dowling...Sue Dowling.' I can see and hear him today. I did not mind his attention, but the Cowans were quite a reserved family and they would get embarrassed and try to restrain his ebullience especially as he grew larger and larger. Johnny would spend hours and hours ripping newspapers into long even strips. It was amazing how regular those strips were.

At secondary school I took what was called Professional which meant that languages such as Latin and French would be part of the curriculum. The other option was Commercial and, as its name implies involved Shorthand and Typing. Susan Cowan took Professional so with our interest in the piano and our neighbourhood proximity we became very good friends. Joan Walters, who took Commercial started to recede although not entirely as when we were age fifteen we travelled down to the South Island together.

Sometimes there were concerts put on at the school and of course Helen Morpeth's regular play productions. On one of these occasions Susan Cowan and I wrote and devised a short skit. It involved me dressing up as a dopey boy and Susan as a glamourous girl. There was a grumpy teacher involved. Helen Morpeth played this role. We made up a puerile tune and it went as follows.

> Dopey boy: 'I called on my sweetheart, her name was Miss Cowan. She was having a bath so she couldn't come down. I said slip on something, come down in a tick. She slipped on the soap, my she did come down quick 'Tra la la la la, Tra la le le le. How would you how would you like to be me?'

> Glamorous girl: 'To a school dance in August he's asked me to go. But unfortunately I had to say no. For he has knock knees and has big googly eyes. I wouldn't be seen dead with that antique prize. Tra la la etc'

> Grumpy teacher: 'Now what's all this nonsense that's going on here? I've told you before from these boys to keep clear. The school is no place for arranging your dates. If it happens again you'll go out through the gates. Tra la la etc'

We wrote and practised this at the Cowan's house and Johnny would listen in, spellbound, chuckling all the time. He latched on to the words the teacher says 'I've told you before' and from that day whenever he saw me I had to sing those words while frowning angrily and using a very grumpy voice. He would laugh until he cried and would continually pester the repetition of these few words sung in that grumpy voice. After half a dozen times someone would intervene and he would be made to stop. I didn't mind in the slightest bit. His life was very limited and if I could give him some pleasure I was willing to do so.

Years later which you will remember vividly Amelia when we were at my parents' house. For some reason they were not there. They were probably at church. It was nighttime when, from outside, we saw and heard a dark shadowy figure stumbling up the driveway. Next minute there was a loud banging at the door and a lot of shouting which sounded faintly familiar. I was very frightened as I thought it was some drunk madman and I had my child to protect. I shouted with all my might. 'Go away, just go away' The person kept banging and shouting and finally I realised that this person was shouting 'Sue Dowling' over and over again. Suddenly it dawned on me that it was Johnny Cowan. He had heard that I was visiting and had lumbered around to see me. By this time he was about six foot three and only just recognisable as the child I had known. I opened the door and Johnny fell upon me.

Chapter 10 - Going to Church
and other religious matters

Dear Amelia and Fionn:

I am not yet returning to the theme of friends as I want to tell you about the exercise of our religion in all its forms. Going to church was like attending live theatre. It had all the elements including drama, a cast of diverse characters, pageantry, music, props and costumes.

There was a variety of events held in the church. The main one was the Mass, but there were also peripheral ones such as Devotions (which was also called Benediction) and the Novena. During the year there were extra events to celebrate a month. For example, May was the month of Mary and March was the month of the Sacred Heart. At the start of these months there were often processions especially in May as devotion to Mary was huge. I loved these processions. We glided around the streets with the statue of the Virgin Mary mounted on a plinth, eyes downcast scattering petals and singing songs whose theme was the Virgin Mary, purity, and of course spotless wombs. The priests were in full regalia. There was lots of incense puffing out of the thurible as the priest rocked it back and forth. There was much tinkling of bells and many candles. What child would not like this spectacle? I also liked Benediction as lots of the hymns were in Latin and therefore mostly incomprehensible but sounded magical to my young ears.

> *Tantum ergo sacramentum veneremu cernui. Et antiquum documentum, novo cedat ritui and*
>
> *O salutaris hostia, quae caeli pandis ostium . Bella remunt hostilia, da robur fer auxiliam*

The ones sung in English were also appealing

> *Sweet sacrament of peace dear home of every heart*
>
> *where restless yearning cease and sorrows all depart.*
>
> *There in thy ear all trustfully* (for a long time I sang 'within thy earhole trustfully')

we tell our tale of misery...

sweet Sacrament of peace, sweet sacrament of peace'.

There were lots of misunderstandings as one listened to the liturgy of the church and the sermons. One which puzzled me a great deal was the Offertory and when I became old enough to read the Missal, I wondered mightily who 'N and N' were. The priest was inviting the congregation to pray for the departed and in the Missal it had the notation 'N and N'. I used to think how lucky 'N and N' were always being prayed for throughout the world. What had they done to deserve this? It was only years later that I realised that 'N and N' stood for the Latin Nomine and that each member of the congregation was invited to mention silently the name of someone who had died. That was a revelation to me. The word jurisdiction often cropped up too whether in a sermon or in some tract or other. For a long time I thought the priest was saying Judith Dixon who was a girl at my school.

The vestments worn during benediction seemed exotic and there was lots of incense and at the end the priest turns and blesses the congregation with an ornate monstrance which has the host inside it. Everyone bows and looks solemn as they are blessed with the body and blood of Christ.

November 2nd was All Souls' Day. On this day the church commemorated all the faithful departed who had had the misfortune to die with lesser sins on their souls and were stuck in Purgatory. At least there was hope for them unlike those who were in Limbo because they had died before being baptised and their cases were hopeless because they were stuck in Limbo for all eternity. These poor creatures were often babies who had died and whose parents had not hurried and had delayed their baptism. For the souls trapped in Purgatory there was hope and November 2nd was their 'big day out'. On this day Catholics spent a lot of time at church going in and out and saying a prayer and gaining a Plenary Indulgence. This remits punishment due to sin and allows these poor trapped creatures to leap up into Heaven. The more times a person went into church, said a prayer, went out again for a few minutes, then back in again for another prayer. It became a bit of a competition as to how many souls on could 'get into heaven' on this day. Other times of the year a person could only get one soul a day out of purgatory but November 2nd,

The Feast of All Souls. it was open slather. It had of course a comic element seeing all these people running in and out of church intent on releasing as many souls as possible. We sang

Oh turn to Jesus Mother turn, and call him by his tenderest name.

*Pray for the Holy Souls who **burn this hour amidst the cleansing flames.***

It may have been this hymn which gave rise to a recurring dream which I had. I was in purgatory. This took the form of long rows of wooden tables with wooden benches upon which countless people sat, doing nothing but sitting. Under the table were gas rings, one for each person. These were constantly alight burning the knees of the sitters. One had to sit here until someone performed enough indulgences or ran in and out of church with you in mind on All Souls' Day.

Easter was a big event in the calendar of the church. It came at the end of Lent, during which we had all given up things we liked. A common question at school was 'What have you given up for Lent?'. Sometimes it was hard to find something as our lives felt quite Spartan anyway. We never had chocolate and seldom had lollies. Maybe we could give up Foxton Fizz which my father brought home sometimes after he had inspected their boiler and the Foxton Fizz makers had given him a crate to take home. He would store it at the back of his large garage under lock and key and dish it out when he was feeling particularly benevolent. We had to stand at the side entrance to the garage miles from where it was stored, not setting a foot in the garage while he jingled his keys and brought it forth and handed it out to his excited children. This was a rare event so was probably not worth giving up for Lent. We could give up my mother's home baking which she did all the time but that felt too hard. Perhaps sleeping without a pillow, but that didn't last as it was far too difficult. Usually one found something but kept it to oneself as it felt quite a private privation. I can remember pretending that I had given up something when I hadn't at all or giving up something for a while then letting it slip.

The Easter rituals began with Palm Sunday which falls on the Sunday before Easter and heralds the beginning of Holy Week, and the last week of Lent. On that day Jesus's triumphal entry into Jerusalem is celebrated. On this day we celebrated with processions and distribution of blessed Palm leaves. The palm leaves we used were picked from the abundant hedge outside the school in Carroll Street. How I loved the smell of these leaves and would sniff this hedge eagerly each day I arrived at school. The next event was Maundy Thursday the next Thursday following Palm Sunday. I always felt the mournful onomatopoeic effect of this word but in fact it comes from the Latin word Mandatum which was a new commandment which Jesus gave his disciples in the upper room during the last Supper when he told them to love one another. This commemorates the 'Washing of the Feet' of the Apostles by Jesus. The Pope in Rome washes the feet of twelve ordinary people, always men. I do not recall any feet washing in St Patrick's in Palmerston North but if it did occur it certainly my mother would not have had her feet washed even though she had provided the church with so many 'heirs to the kingdom of Heaven'. After that day there is Good Friday which is a big day as it is the day Jesus was crucified. The purple cloths covering the 14 depictions of the story of Jesus's crucifixion are removed. In our church we attended the Stations of the Cross where a gaggle of priests, whose vestments were always purple or black, and altar boys moved around the fourteen pictures placed around the church portraying the events in the Passion of Christ and singing mournful chants in Latin.

Easter Saturday is a quiet day where anticipation is in the air. We all got Easter eggs and of course time away from school. Jesus is in the tomb ready to rise and the next day when he does there is great celebration. There is a full Latin Mass, white vestments, much bell ringing, and singing of joyful Easter Hymns with words of joy and hope.

Hail redeemer king divine,

priest and lamb the throne is thine.

King whose reign will never cease .

Lord of everlasting peace.

Angels saints and nations sing.

Praise be Jesus Christ our King.
Lord of life earth sky and sea.
King of love on Calvary' and
'By the first bright Easter Day.
When the stone was rolled away.
By the cloud of living light, that received thee out of sight.

Easter was the highlight and even surpassed Christmas in its importance on the liturgical calendar but there were all sorts of other religious rituals carried out beside the Mass. The main one was the Novena, which happened on a Saturday evening. My mother always insisted that someone from our family attended and sometimes the resistance from us was quite fierce but eventually someone succumbed to her pleas. As a virtual sub-branch of the Catholic Church we had to have a representative attend all these events. The Novena had its origins in the Miracle of Fatima, when three peasant children Lucia, Francisco and Jacinta reported to have had a vision of a lady luminously lit up and standing on a bush in Fatima, Portugal in 1917. This happened six times. They were given three secrets which involved hell, World War one and World War two.

The version we were told as children was that the third secret would be revealed in 1960. The pope at the time when the secret was given to him was Pius 12th and, when he opened it and read it, he cried so much and for such a long time that deep furrows formed in his cheeks. The gist of the secret was that, if Russia was not converted back to Christianity and the country did not consecrate itself to the Immaculate Heart of Mary, the world would end in 1960.

And so we lived with this terrifying foreboding. I was 15 in 1960. My mother was in the throes of her severe and unending nervous breakdown and I was waiting for the world to end. This was the equivalent of the threat of nuclear war which hung over your generation Amelia and climate change which hangs over your generation Fionn. The arrival of the Novena gave rise to a positive catalogue of new hymns all devoted to the Virgin Mary. The emphasis in these hymns moved away from bodily carnage to a softer message which was nevertheless just as visceral and the themes of purity and virginity were foremost. Once again the trowel was used to ram home the message. Who wrote these I know not but some distorted mind must have had a hand in it. Here is a sample

Oh Purest of creatures, sweet mother sweet maid.

The one spotless womb wherein Jesus was laid.

His home and his hiding place once were in thee.

He was won by thy shining sweet star of the sea'...

(and later in the same hymn)

earth gave him one lodging, was deep in thy breast.

The recurring themes were obsessively preoccupied with wombs and breasts which had to be spotless of course. If Catholic womanhood hadn't got the message by then they 'had eyes that see not and ears that hear not'. The Novena audience however, was small and select and I never once saw any of my fellow school friends in the congregation. Part of the ritual was to read out Petitions asking the Virgin Mary for favours. My mother always put in one or more petitions and we always knew which ones were hers. The favourite one was 'for peace and harmony in the home' but alas, the Virgin Mary was deaf to her pleas.

Father Peyton was called the Rosary Priest and he set out on a crusade to promote devotion to the Virgin Mary. He coined the phrase 'The family who prays together, stays together'. He travelled far and wide including New Zealand and had a huge crusade gathering in the Palmerston North Showgrounds in 1954. Hundreds of people turned up and said the rosary and sang hymns to the Virgin Mary.

Oh Queen of the family rosary,

we dedicate our homes to thee

and pray aloud each special bead

to supplicate our every need' and

'Our Lady of Fatima,

we come on bended knee.

To beg your intercession for peace and unity.

Dear Mary won't you show us the right and shining way.

We pledge our love and offer you a rosary each day.

Of course we all attended this rally and from that day vowed to say the Rosary daily which of course we did without fail. At the rally my father was invited to lead a decade of the Rosary over the loudspeaker and he was assigned a sorrowful mystery. It was probably because he had proved himself so undeniably in assisting to swell the world with Catholics that he was chosen, but without my mother I am sure his adherence to this religion would have been much less ardent. Every night at 7pm we were summoned to kneel in the living room and recite the five decades of the rosary. There were three Mysteries. The Joyful Mysteries, the Sorrowful Mysteries and the Glorious Mysteries and we used one of these as the theme according to which day of the week it was. It remains a mystery to me as to why they were called mysteries. We prefaced each decade of the rosary with an offering for some unfortunate person amongst our family or friends in the hope that our collective prayer would aid this person in some way back to health or away from the sinful life they were leading.

We all owned a pair of rosary beads which were all piled up on the mantelpiece. There was a statue of the Virgin Mary there too. The quality of this statue was a cut above those produced by Sister Colette but in due course there was a chip off her nose. Someone must have knocked her while dusting. If the phone rang during the rosary there was a general dive for the door to answer it in a bid to escape. My mother always added what we called 'trimmings' depending what month it was. In May she added the litany of the Virgin Mary and in March the Litany of the Sacred Heart. My mother would make an invocation and we would reply 'pray for us' Some examples of these remain embedded in my head even today. How would a child make head or tail of such things as 'singular vessel of devotion' 'mystical rose',' tower of David', 'Arc of the covenant',' tower of ivory',' house of gold' morning star, refuge of sinners', 'comfort of the afflicted' and on and on it went and of course there were the usual reference to chastity, purity and virginity. The Virgin Mary set a high bar for struggling Catholic girls and many if not most fell by the wayside.

The Litany to the Sacred Heart was even more incomprehensible The reply to these invocations such as 'Heart of Jesus abyss of all virtues' was 'have mercy on us'. 'Heart of Jesus abode of all justice and love' and

'Heart of Jesus burning furnace of charity'. For all this incomprehensible verbiage I still found a great fascination for the language which again did not require understanding to savour. My mother once asked my cousin Mary, when she was visiting, if her family said the rosary every night. 'Yes,' she replied 'but we might as well be saying bucket and brush, bucket and brush'. I will never forget the look on my mother's face as she stared down at this little rebel and took issue with this reductive analysis of such a pious undertaking. I do not think my mother rated Mary as a good girl from that day on.

So we pedalled to the church week after week, sometimes day after day. In fact it, could be said that we almost lived there. At school we went to funerals all the time of unknown Catholics who had died. Our crocodile formations would snake down Fitchett Street, across Featherstone Street, through the Marist Brothers' school and on to the church where Mr Hickey the undertaker, who looked like a corpse in waiting would preside over the rituals while we sang

Agonising Heart of Jesus

Agonising Heart of Jesus

Have pity on the dying

Have mercy on the dead.

Eternal rest Grant to him/her Oh Lord

And make perpetual light shine upon him/her

May he/she rest in peace

May he/she rest in peace

My mother would not let up on the absolute necessity of someone from the family attending every ritualistic event on offer. But the rich panoply of characters who attended church provided much entertainment and I watched the antics of these people year after year. There was Mr and Mrs Cronin who went to the early mass on Sunday. He would march up to the church to the front pew. Behind tripped his stout wife whose painted face was a sight to behold. For each one of his manly strides she made two or even three little skips in order to keep up. His chivalry did not extend to slowing down so that she could keep up, but as soon as his destination was reached chivalry came to the fore. He swept back extended his arm in a wide sweep to guide her into the seat but before she did he nimbly placed two cushions on the hard wooden pew so that her knees received a soft landing. He then knelt beside her, made a large and exaggerated sign of the cross and prepared to boom any 'amens' or 'pray for us' when called upon to do so. Later when I thought of him and read Dicken's *Hard Times* I could not help calling to mind Josiah Bounderby. This character was a pompous, arrogant and successful factory owner who constantly claimed to be a self-made man. He is eventually revealed as a complete sham and in true Dicken's style his hypocrisy is finally mercilessly exposed.

Then there were the two Cavanagh sisters who provided endless entertainment. They always wore tweed suits and brogues (always the same ones) and thick Lyle stockings. They always brought their two dogs to church. These dogs had to stay in the car of course but there were never windows left open so the windows of their car were always fogged up and bedecked with dog slather. I remember feeling slightly sick if I passed close to these two women as the stale smell of dog was always on them. One of these women was stout and the other very thin. The thin one had an incredibly long face at the top of which two small, wizened eyes sat. She looked to me as though she did not have enough skin to cover her face and which meant her complexion had a stretched look. Her hair was wiry and stiff and looked as if shampooing was not a frequent event. She always wore a brown felt hat from which this hair protruded around the edges.

The other Miss Cavanagh was stout and was a cross between Fred Flintstone and Scooby Doo. She had a square face, the bottom part of which was wide with a lantern jaw. Her hair was completely hidden under a larger brown felt hat and she two had the odour of dog upon her. They always sat in the same place in church, so it was rare to be within smelling distance. My sister Pauline and I dubbed these two 'Monny and Sconny'. Another pair of sisters who fascinated us we called 'French Doll and Coat hanger' as we did not know their real names. All their garments had wide and unforgiving shoulder pads which gave the impression that their waists were stick thin. One was dark and other fair and the fair one had a pretty but lifeless heavily made-up face. Today we would have accused her of having endless botox sessions. Their hair was permed to the point that the bits that stuck out from under their hats was as solid as a rock, so there must have been a great deal of hair spray involved. They were professional dressmakers and wore tailored suits and were as neat as two pins. And one knew too that they were as clean as two whistles.

Then there were the single men who had become self-appointed ushers. The most notable was Leo Denham who seemed to think he was the concert master of the whole show. He was shabbily dressed and was without doubt a drinker as he had a bulbous red nose with broken veins crisscrossing his face. He would rush about and marshal people into their pews with great nervous energy making sure that wasted space was filled up, often by unwilling participants in this organising frenzy. When communion time came he would lurk at the top of the centre aisle marshalling people to the altar rails so that no gap was left unfilled. He had been seen to lunge forward and fill a space himself if there was no other candidate and stick out his tongue in the nick of time like a frog catching a fly. Today some diagnostic label would be attached to this behaviour but then no such definitions were available and 'stark raving mad' covered a multiple of conditions. Then there was Lionel Orme a tall gaunt figure who also took it upon himself to guide the laity to their pews. He was a bit half-hearted in this endeavour as his energy levels were about the same as Bern Spelman's and his body competed with the aforementioned in that he moved as one piece and resembled a wax statue temporarily brought to life for the occasion.

But the comic 'tour de force' was Mamie Spelman. Mamie had taken it upon herself to play the organ at times when the official organist was unavailable or at the Saturday Novena or Devotions. The official organists were Cora Bartlett and her sister Beryl. They were both good musicians. Beryl taught the violin and Cora the piano and they trained the church choir, which I joined for a while after I left school. My father was heard to make the unkind remarks 'You could put a plate on Beryl Bartlett's bottom and it would not fall off'. It was true that she had the most unusual form and her bottom certainly did resemble a shelf. Cora and Beryl left the field open to another candidate for Devotions and the Saturday Novena and into this void stepped Mamie Spelman.

Devotions were just another device to make my mother feel guilty that she was not attending and were held on various weeknights. They consisted of lots of prayers and hymns. Here is where Mamie triumphed. She could neither sing nor play the organ but she did both with such gusto and enthusiasm that one listened in disbelief at her confidence. She played the organ in such a way that all the individual notes completely joined up and made a blanket of sound where the actual tune was nowhere to be found. Her singing was a cross between a hen about to lay too many eggs and a chicken in the throes of being slaughtered. To add to this, she was short and could not reach the pedals of the organ so that in order to reach them she had to wobble her stout rotund body from side to side. The organ stool literally groaned under this challenge. Not only was one rewarded with the cacophony of appalling sound but the added theatrical bonus of a show.

So, when my cousin Mary came to stay her first request was 'Can we go to church and hear Mamie sing'. My mother was suspicious of this burst of piety but did not demur, so off we went on our bikes heavily armed with handkerchiefs to stuff in our mouths when the time came. Mamie only had to mount the organ stool and start wobbling and Mary and I would be off, shaking and shuddering and choking on our handkerchiefs until the final chord. Mary has an infectious laugh and can, even to this day, set me off and as a child this laugh was always ready to respond to anything even mildly amusing. But with Mamie the amusement was first class, and I had even noticed the priest sometimes struggling to stay appropriately grave in the face of this sheer comedy.

But the church also held perils for me especially as I grew into adolescence. When nylon stockings came to be part of my life so did the anxiety that one's seams were crooked and worse that the stockings had become wrinkled. The greatest fear was that there was a ladder in one's stockings which no amount of nail polish had stopped spreading. All these things were crimes in the canon of fashion law in the 1950's. But that most alarming fear of all was that one's suspender belt would not hold and everything would fall down around one's ankles. All these garments were seriously uncomfortable but this was not considered ever or questioned and later, when one graduated from suspender belts to Easies or corsets, they too could be very uncomfortable. So, when tights came in which did not require things to clip one's stockings to, a universal sigh of relief went up I am sure.

Chapter 11 – Music and Music teachers

Dear Amelia and Fionn:

The theme of education is a broad one so when I speak of music in my life it is inextricably tied up with education. I have already recounted how musical my mother was. She also started all of us on the piano before consigning us to the mixed bag of music teacher nuns. My mother was always a patient teacher so starting to learn the piano was a good experience. There was the added bonus of have thirty minutes of one's mother to one's self, which was a rare thing. When it was my turn to leave her and be taught by the nuns, there were two choices. Sister Michael or Sister Sophie. Sister Michael was very old, probably at least in her eighties. She was always welcoming and called everyone darling, but she always repeated that word as she greeted you with the salutation 'hello darling darling darling'. That was her hallmark. I do not think she was a very teacher and was probably past it, but she was the teacher of choice in our family.

Unluckily for me the dice landed on Sister Sophie and the dread kicked in immediately. Here was a forerunner of Sister Clothilde with exactly the same cold grey eyes and pasty damp skin. When she was in a good mood, which Sister Clothilde never was, her eyes could temporarily sparkle a bit and she could be quite jolly but she was mercurial. 'When she was good, she was very very good. When she was bad she was horrid'. She absolutely terrified me so that music lessons became an ordeal to be dreaded. I begged my mother to let me have Sister Michael but my appeals fell on deaf ears so into the pirhana infested waters I swam clutching my leather music bag. Each week as one walked into the music room the person leaving and the person entering would whisper to one another. 'What sort of mood is she in?' This would decide one's anxiety levels as one approached. Sister Sophie was an unhappy woman. When reflecting on these days I have come to the conclusion that she was probably menopausal as she sweated a lot and she always seemed hot and bothered. No doubt the cumbersome black habit did not help and one drags up some sympathy from some depleted source if that was the case.

104

Nevertheless, I proceeded to do music exams and theory exams under her tutelage and passed usually with merit. The piano exams were another source of great anxiety. The examiners always came from England and were either from the Royal School of Music or the Trinity College of Music. The RSM was considered more difficult than Trinity College as it was a bigger organisation and being so could travel more widely so by and large we sat the exams belonging to that body. Some terrifying examiner came to Palmerston North annually, sat in Sister Sophie's room and proceeded to order the hapless examinee to play certain scales, execute four learned piano pieces and then be subjected to a series of ear tests. Once we got to the ear tests I had started to relax as I actually enjoyed these and often got full marks for this segment of the exam. One always knew that Sister Sophie was within earshot adding another level of angst to the whole process. The examiners were always men and, by and large, kind and pleasant so, if one could get over the perception of being at the centre of this person's attention and that one was being tested, the ordeal was watered down a bit. I quite religiously got merit for my piano exams which was right in the middle of the field. The top was Honours and the bottom was Pass. I was always happy with that position.

Musical theory was taught hand in hand with the practical. We went every Saturday morning and sat in Sister Sophie's music room where we were instructed in all aspects of the subject. There is one event which stands out and nearly qualifies as a 'Flag pole' moment but not quite because the element of surprise was missing. It did not 'come out of the blue' but built up gradually to a crescendo. We were learning time signatures and their values. I was 11 and in Standard 5. At school we were learning fractions where of course a line is put between the numbers. My mistake was to put a line between the time signature numbers as one does with fractions. Sister Sophie would walk around looking at our work. Time and time again she scored a red pencil through my work and told me to do that again. I had no idea what I was doing wrong and continued to put a line between the numbers. Around she came and with increasing vengeance put a red line between my time signatures. I was absolutely perplexed and getting increasingly upset. I tried making one of the numbers big and the other small as I knew I had the answer right. Back she came and higher went the volume of her anger. By this time I had began to sob quietly as I had no idea what I was doing wrong. My sister Pauline who was sitting opposite me desperately tried to mouth and gesticulate what I was doing wrong but by then my distress was so great I was deaf and blind to her attempts at sign language.

Finally Sister Sophie was in a blind rage and I was an emotional mess. She finally screamed 'take out the line between the numbers'. The penny dropped and I did so. Calm descended except in my distraught bosom and I continued to cry uncontrollably. When we went home I told my mother and redoubled my attempts to transfer to Sister Michael to no avail. And so music lessons proceeded for a few years. Suddenly after about 4 years of Sister Sophie at the age of twelve I was transferred to Sister Columbiere. I do not know what happened to Sister Sophie. Perhaps she exploded. Calm seas at last. Sister Columbiere was amiable, kind and warm. She was a large woman with beautiful skin and soft blue eyes. I started to like my music lessons but alas she was not a good music teacher as she did not have an authoritarian bone in her body, so I started to slacken on music practice at home. She taught me until I went to St Mary's at the age of fifteen and fell into the arms of Sister Cecily.

Sister Cecily was quite kind but had an aura of repressed fierceness about her which I was always wary of. She was quite a good teacher but without knowing it I longed for the good teacher combined with the kind warm person. Finally this combination happened in the form of Sister Michelle but this was much later and so I must return to sister Cecily. She had very skin and blue eyes which did not sparkle much and in fact were quite cold. She always smelt of a sickly talcum powder. However, she never lost her temper but was coldly intolerant of playing which was not up to scratch so I was always on tenterhooks. My sister Pauline scored the best music teacher at St Mary's and it was fitting that she did as she got the lion's share of the musical talent in our family and with Sister Loreto she had landed in the right place. She had large octave stretching hands like my mother and considerable talent on the two musical levels of singing and the piano and with Sister Loreto she had come home to roost as she was a superb music teacher and Pauline was a prodigious talent. Sister Loreto had been a childhood friend of my mother's and had been known as Girlie Gibbs a name which has gone down as a moniker in parts of our family as you will know Amelia.

There is however one event which warrants recording as it again teeters on the edge of being a 'flagpole moment' but again just escapes as it was a gradual and predictable event and did not come suddenly upon me. We were having a concert in our school hall and I was due to play a duet called *Rondo Alla Turca* by Mozart with a girl called Helen Bergin who later went on to become a nun. At the same time I was practising hard for my grade seven piano exam, which was a week after the concert, so I was neglecting the practice of Rondo Alla Turca. I went to see Sister Cecily and pleaded with her to let me off the hook but she was unable to me persuaded. The day of the concert approached and as it did my nervous condition deteriorated. We were not allowed to have the music so it had to be done by heart. As I was in the schola, which was a special group of singers at St Mary's trained by Sister Winifred I was on the stage for the duration of the concert as the Schola was singing.

As the time of the duet approached I got more and more terrified and clung to the girl next to me who was called Rosemary Hishon, a kind daygirl. She was whispering reassurances to me and squeezing my hand. Finally the moment came and we stepped forward and sat at the piano. Helen Bergin nodded and began to play the treble part of the piece. I did not start and dared not glance at the front row of nuns one of whom was hissing 'Start'. Helen Bergin nodded and started again. I stumbled a few notes, she carried on tinkling away with the treble part of the piece while I tried fruitlessly to intervene and connect the base. When this failed, I crashed my hands down onto the piano and ran from the stage. Is this not the performer's nightmare? I ran from the school hall and sat down in one of the classrooms and waited for the tsunami of reaction from Sister Cecily.

The concert continued. Surprisingly Sister Cecily's wrath was expressed but nothing like as bad as I had expected. She probably knew that I had asked to be let off the hook and that it was partly her fault. But wrath did come from a quarter and that quarter was Sister Juliana. She taught the theory of music and the syllabus for School Certificate music. She was a hopeless teacher and simply could not impart information clearly. She had taught me the year before for School Certificate music

107

and I had failed dismally getting the lowest mark of all my subjects 46%. In part this was my state of mind but in large part it was her bad teaching. And it wasn't helped by the mid-exam earthquake I have already mentioned. She was tall and good looking. Her personality was brittle and she had been afflicted with an overdose of verbal sibilance, which is usually the hallmark of a flabby personality in my experience. Sister Julianna absolutely went for me accusing me of all sorts of deficiencies the main one it seems was that 'you have no poise', a mortal sin in her opinion. Does a sixteen-year-old whose parameters of life were as limited as mine have poise? Does such a quality not belong to a finishing school where poise is acquired at great expense? Does one not need 'poise' role models?' Strangely enough her opinion did not matter to me and everyone else was kind and sympathetic especially Rosemary Hishon who had been privy to my mounting terror.

I was charged with lack of poise a few years later as I was about to embark for London. Uncle Ro happened to call in at our house as I was doing my final packing. 'Susie leaves for London tomorrow' said my father. Uncle Ro looked at me pointedly and said 'well, I hope some overseas travel helps you to gain some poise'. There it was again that horrible word poise. If it means being graceful and elegant with good deportment then no amount of travel is going to help was my secret thought.

The *Alla Turca* incident caused me to recall another 'moment musicaux' when I was playing in the Palmerston North piano competitions in the Town Hall, another dreaded but non-negotiable event. I was playing a piano duo with Helen Lavin. It was Debussy's Claire de Lune. Halfway through I flicked over the page and the entire piece of music landed on the lap of a woman in the front row. I continued to the end as I did know this piece off by heart. I never won any prizes in these events but the school had to send a certain number of 'lambs to the slaughter' as part of keeping up the credibility of its musical reputation.

The best musical experience I had was being a member of the Schola at St Mary's in Wellington. This was a specially chosen group of the best singers from the school. The musical director was Sister Winifred. I was allowed to join this group when I went to St Mary's in the 5th Form. It was probably because my sister Pauline was such a good singer that there was the assumption that I was too. I loved being part of this group. Sister Winifred was talented and musically enquiring and we were taught a wide variety of material some of which was far from mainstream for a girls' choir to access. An example of this was The Rig Veda which is an ancient Indian collection of Vedic Sanskrit hymns. Initially it is not accessible to the ear but with time and repetition we came to love it even though it seemed discordant at first. Upon exposure the harmonies and the words became compelling and satisfying.

We learned a wide variety of choral material including The Ceremony of Carols by Benjamin Brittain, lots of Irish English and Welsh songs, including 'Silent of Moyle be the roar of thy water' and

Bring me said David the harp I adore.

I long ere death calls me to play it once more' and

'On the Banks of Allen Waters when the sweet spring tide is full,

stood the miller's lovely daughter fairest of them all' and

'In Hans old mill his three black cats,

watch the bins for the thieving rats.

I loved all this material and we gave many concerts. Sister Winifred had a lovely calm and inclusive nature and an even temper. She herself gained much satisfaction from music and had a lovely voice herself. She was also an accomplished pianist. She was always ready to laugh and never scolded or diminished any of us. As a result she extracted the best from all of us. For me The Schola was the highlight of any musical endeavours I pursued at any time of my life.

Later though when I moved to Wellington I joined the St Mary of the Angel's choir. This was a wonderful experience as the choirmaster Maxwell Fernie was an accomplished organist and choir master. He had previously been an organist at Westminster Cathedral and he had a talent for getting the very best out of the array of talent in front of him. My sister Pauline was one of the stars of this choir and was always chosen as the contralto soloist when the need arose. During my time in this choir we made three recordings two of which were polyphony and another of Christmas music. On this record to my surprise he chose me to sing about three lines as the contralto soloist. I used to try and imitate Pauline's sound which was strong and distinctive. This imitation must have worked to a limited degree. My brother-in-law Louis Morganti, who was married to my eldest sister MaryClare, was a leading tenor in this choir. He had a beautiful voice and listening to these recordings today I can hear his beautiful sound strongly permeating from the solo group and I feel deep sadness that he died so young at the age of 49 and even deeper sadness that I was in England when this happened and could not be there to say goodbye to him or help my sister and her distraught family. He gave so much pleasure to so many people with his beautiful soaring pure tenor voice and his kind, gentle soft nature.

The enjoyment of this choir was diluted by my anxiety and almost fear of Maxwell Fernie. He could be cruelly blunt and would mark certain people for ridicule. These people were often plain women and he would never do this to an attractive young woman many of whom were in love with him. My self-consciousness and anxiety was at its height at this time for many reasons which will be explained in due season so I was always in a state of nervousness which I am sure he took note of. I had had an experience with Maxwell Fernie when I was in the 6th form at St Mary's. It was the year of the 100 year jubilee and there was great celebration including many concerts. Eileen Duggan who was a renowned poet and journalist wrote a special piece for the occasion and Maxwell Fernie set it to music.

Over a noble heart there is great measure.

Its sun is honour with peace above.

Such was the soul whence sprang your works of mercy.

Her queenly beauty lives in your love.

In pain and darkness the poor and the dying

find your blessed comfort aids them to endure

On it went like this as a tribute to Catherine McAuley the founder of the Sisters of Mercy. At the time I was not impressed either with the words or the music, but of course I kept my counsel. When Maxwell Fernie came to the school to practise with us for the great jubilee day I was assigned to meet him and bring him into the school hall. It was on one of these occasions that he started to call me 'string bag'. I am not sure what he meant by this, but can attempt an explanation. He saw before him a tallish thin plain self-conscious girl, whose movements were fast and possibly jerky and whose speech was rapid and possibly shaky. After all I was meeting the great man and before great men one bowed and scraped and even quailed. I am sure he would have preferred to be met by a nubile nymph who would have been more to his taste. I guess a string bag is flaccid and full of holes and when unfilled is completely limp. But what he possibly failed to appreciate is that a string bag is capacious and has the potential to be filled and carry more goods than many other handheld bags. I am sure I am reading too much into this but I also know that today I would return the compliment with a jibe about his quite severely pock marked face. Of course, I would never do that but at least I can fantasize.

The last music teacher I ever had was Sister Michelle and she was the best. Music lessons were fun with her. She was always light-hearted and happy and there was always laughter involved. She had quick movements and had a lovely face and was always as neat as a pin in everything she did. The best thing however, is that she played recordings of the pieces of music I was learning played by the best people. Suddenly one heard how it could sound and strove in that direction. What a revelation. During this time I sat Grade 7 theory of music and got the astounding mark of 93%. There was amazement all 'round and Sister Michelle even remarked that perhaps the marker had transposed the numbers and it should have been 37%. I did not take umbrage at this remark at all and was inclined to agree as my domestic life was difficult during this time and did not leave much time to prepare.

I cannot conclude this account of my music in my life without mentioning the influence my sister Pauline and my sister-in-law Pauline had on me. Pauline Gardiner, as we often call her, married my brother Tony. She was, and still is, a beautiful person both inside and out. She is a very good pianist and singer and so is my sister Pauline. They were both studying music at the time. When she and my sister Pauline set up a flat together in Wellington, which I was part of briefly, Pauline had brought her piano from Hastings. They often played and sang around this piano and I joined in. During this time I learned a great number of Schubert Lieder which I can remember today and later when I learned German I started to learn some of them in that language. They sang that beautiful Schubert song *An Die Musik* and lots of arias from Handel's oratorios particularly *The Messiah*, from Haydn's *The Creation*, and English and Scottish folk songs. I loved these sessions and owe my love and knowledge of this music to these experiences.

Chapter 12 – Being Parked Out.

Dear Amelia and Fionn:

I have alluded to, and even described in detail above, how my desperate overwhelmed parents sometimes assigned us to other families, often for long stretches of time . Many of these people were our relatives, but not always. I have related the experience of being sent to my Grandmother's home in Avon Street in Island Bay Wellington and of course being sent to the Fullers just down the road from where we lived. During my childhood my uncle Barry and Aunty Cassie played a huge part in my care and later in my brother Joseph's care.

Because my cousin Mary was a year younger than me it made sense to consign me to these relatives. For me this was a fortunate choice. Mary and I by and large got on well. She was the only girl in a family of four boys. This meant two things. One she had a confidence I completely lacked and, being the only girl, she always had new clothes, which I seldom had. In our family we even had to share pants (called knickers these days) and sometimes there simply was not a clean pair to be had, so on went what we had worn yesterday and probably the day before. The O'Regan household was fearsomely busy but no one ever shouted. Often at night we would hear my father shouting at my mother no doubt concerning some incident which had occurred during the day. Her replies would be muffled but these nocturnal conversations caused us all to hold our breath until silence once again returned. Not breathing is a habit I have had to unlearn and the genesis of this habit is the anxiety experienced during the many discordant occurrences in my young life.

Aunty Cassie could be brusque but she never stopped working. She was always kind to me and in time I know she grew fond of me and I of her, as she told me in her later years when I went to visit her, which I always did when I was in Wellington. She once said to me 'Susie, you have the nicest nature in your family'. I liked her saying that, but I was cognisant of the fact that she knew me well, perhaps better than the others. When she was on her deathbed, someone asked her about her life. She replied 'It was arduous' and so it was. There were five children in the family, four boys and Mary. The boys were nice to me but we largely ignored one another although John was consigned to take Mary and me to the Museum every holidays which he dutifully did. Apart from Mary I had little to do with the boys subsequently except for Mark who was the youngest. Much later when he was assigned to sit at the Auckland High Court he and his wife Nicky joined my book club. He has subsequently been appointed to the Supreme Court and has been knighted for his services to the NZ judiciary as was his father. I discovered during my time working in the legal environment that he is held in high esteem amongst his colleagues, not just for his sharp mind but also for his warm personality. Mary too rose to great heights. In 1985 she was appointed to establish and head the brand new New Zealand Ministry of Woman's Affairs. She was the first woman in New Zealand to head a Ministry let alone face the daunting task of setting up such an organisation. She did this task with great skill and courage and during her working life did much good work advocating on behalf of women in the workplace. As far as I am aware she has not been offered any accolades in the honour's list for this pioneering work.

To the O'Regan's I went most holidays. This may have been a bit onerous for Mary, as she had other friends who needed a look in but it seemed to work. Sometimes Mary came to Palmerston to stay with us. She was always larger than life and apart from our mandatory visit to church to hear Mamie Spelman, there are two incidents I can recall. One was when she was sweeping the kitchen with a terrible hairless broom. She was banging and crashing her way around the kitchen when my father shouted angrily at her to stop that racket. 'Well' she said 'if you had a broom with hairs on it I would' and continued banging and crashing. Soon after a new broom appeared. Another more memorable incident was when she was trying to get to the window seat to sit and eat dinner. Instead of sliding in she jumped and went straight through the wooden window seat, which my father had just finished making the week before. There was a gaping hole and a sharp intake of breath all round as we all waited for the outbreak of World War 3 and the furore came in no small measure.

This followed on from an incident where a vinegar bottle had gone through the bathroom basin. We used vinegar on our hair as it was supposed to make it shiny. In this incident my mother desperately tried to get it replaced before my father returned home. Memory does not favour me with the outcome of that incident but I am sure she did not manage to accomplish that, but thet basin was not fixed for a long time. The bathroom was always used as a temporary punishment venue for bad behaviour. During one such incarceration, Rolly kicked through the wooden casing surrounding the bath which my father had recently constructed presumably to maximise the heat in the bath water. These incidents illustrate my father's intense frustration as it always fell on him to fix all these breakages.

But Mary took such incidents as falling through the window seat completely in her stride which I always marvelled at as had the 'boot been on the other foot', and this had been me at their house, I would have been completely undone but then the reaction would have been more muted. Uncle Barry also worked hard in his legal practice. He would sit at the end of the table at the evening meal and crack jokes, most of which were lost on me. I have also been told that he cracked a lot of jokes when he was on the bench. He always took particular notice of me as I think he realised that I was permanently homesick no matter where I was. He used to single me out by singing 'Suzanna's a Funicle Man'. I had no idea that this was an old American folk song which involved grunting like a pig and squeaking like a sow, but I knew it was his way of making me feel included and I remember feeling grateful to him for this attention.

Also resident at the Clyde Street house in Island Bay was Aunty Cassie's father John O'Donnell. He was a permanent fixture in the corner of the large sitting room and only seemed to get up to go to the toilet. He was no blood relation to me as he was my father's stepfather. In fact it is generally accepted that Grandad O'Donnell could have been kinder to the three fatherless boys he inherited when he married Mary Dowling. He did not adopt her children and in fact did not favour them with the bounty he could have. However, when he died and left no inheritance to my father and his brothers, Aunty Cassie with her legendary generosity shared her legacy and my father was able to buy the black shiny Velox Vauxhall which was his pride and joy.

'Don't slam the bloody doors' rings in my ears to this day as he tried to preserve this treasure in all its pristine glory. This car generally impressed us after the horrible green van which belonged to the government and was not allowed to be used for family jaunts. But for Aunty Cassie Grandad O'Donnell added to her domestic burden. I suppose it was thought to be her duty. I have an abiding memory of her carrying his commode up the hall every morning to be emptied. I am not sure what other duties she had to perform behind the closed door of his bedroom. Our family called him Granddad O'Donnell as he was the second husband of my father's mother. The first husband having met his untimely death in an accident when he was buried alive in a gravel pit when my father was three years old. The main memory I have of him is a ditty he endlessly repeated 'I had a little dog and his name was Buff. I took him up town for a box of snuff. He broke the box and spilt the snuff. Don't you think my story's sad enough?' Later when the O'Regan household got a dog there was of course no choice but to name him Buff.

I have already recounted how Mary and I spent these holidays constantly visiting our cousin Dorothy around the corner, skating up and down Avon Street, which had smooth concrete and probably ruining Krause's hedge by sitting on it and making huge holes in it. At one stage Dorothy had a boyfriend called Geoff Dykes who used to like to take her out for jaunts in his Morris Minor car. Dorothy was always eager to take me too and I would sit perkily in the backseat while Geoff Dykes was probably fuming in the front seat. I am sure he wanted Dorothy to herself and maybe had a romantic plan to 'park up' somewhere but Dorothy was not so keen and used me as buffer against such schemes. Later when the O'Regans built a holiday home in Raumati I went there and swam the summer away. When I think how hard Auntie Cassie worked to provide sustenance for all and sundry I am breathless at her energy and the demands put upon her. I cannot recall her ever sitting down or swimming or relaxing in any way, but she probably did.

There was one incident which marred one of these visits. Mary and I were sleeping in a tent on the lawn in front of the house. One morning as we were getting dressed Mary said 'I suppose this is one of Helen Lavin's castoffs'. It was of course, and it was far too big for me and the shoulder seams were half way down my arms. It was a flowery pattern and I can see it today as I saw it then, shapeless and ill-fitting. How I hated that dress, but I had to wear what was on offer without demur. Mary had touched on a nerve. I burst into tears. I was probably tired, definitely homesick as the summer holidays are long and I, as usual, had no idea when I was going home or how my mother was, even if she was home. I packed my things in my suitcase, and set off down the road to go I knew not where. My intention was to find a Newman's bus which I hoped would transport me to Palmerston North and once there I would walk home to Beresford Street to find I knew not what. So off I marched determinedly clutching my worldly possessions.

I had not gone far when a car slowed down beside me. It was Aunty Cassie asking me to get in and come back. 'No' I replied 'I am going home'. Nothing would induce me to get into that car. This was quite an assertive thing for me to do, as I was usually biddable and obedient, so it is a measure of my desperation to go home and see what was happening that I stuck to me guns. Away she went and ten minutes later the neighbour's car slowed down beside me. These people were called Mr and Mrs Souness and they were good friends of the O'Regan family. They asked me to get in promising me that I could stay with them overnight and that the next day they would take me to the Newman's bus for the return journey. I reluctantly climbed in as long as the terms were adhered to which they were. This incident did not mar my relationship with the O'Regan family in any way and is probably not even remembered, although on my last visit to London I visited Peter O'Regan who had remembered and asked me about it which surprised me.

Mary always stuck up for me if required to do so. Her hallmark as a human being is a strong sense of fairness and social justice and she is terminally generous. At the house in Clyde Street there was a huge linen cupboard into which one could walk. One day Mary and I were in there when I did a terrible fart which absolutely stunk the cupboard out and probably contaminated the linen within it. As luck would have it, Aunty Cassie had cause to go in there soon afterwards. She came storming out demanding to know who it was who had violated this clean environment. Mary looked at me and saw my stricken face. 'I did' she said. My gratitude knew no bounds. Aunty Cassie was annoyed and promised a good dose of castor oil. I was so grateful to Mary and happy to escape the administration of this horrible remedy.

Another venue where I was 'parked out' on several occasions was the Home for Wayward Girls run by the Sisters of the Good Shepherd at Te Horo on the Kapiti Coast. This convent and reform school was situated in the country. It was a beautiful setting with a convent, a chapel, and dormitory buildings for the 'wayward girls'. Let me say from the outset that none of these girls was wayward. They were simply neglected both emotionally and physically. By and large they were young and vulnerable and, while I was there, I befriended one or two of them and liked them a lot. How did I get to go to such a place?

My mother had become friendly with the Sisters of the Good Shepherd congregation because she spread her religious net far and wide. She probably sent them donations. As a result they latched on to her and she latched on to them. I would be put on the Newman's bus in Palmerston North and would alight outside the gate of the Convent. As the bus approached Big Mother would hove into view and the bus driver would know to stop for me to alight. The regime at the HFWG was rigorous. We rose to a bell at 6am and fell to our knees at our bedside and uttered a morning prayer. After breakfast we did endless chores but I was allowed some leaway as I was not 'wayward!' One of the things I liked to do was to go into the chapel and play the organ. I had no idea how to play an organ but would make things up and loved doing it as the sound was so fulsome and could sound impressive even if it wasn't.

They had amongst their household a lay woman called Phyllis Niblett. She had wanted to become a member of the congregation but was rejected for reasons of which I am unsure. Phyllis was Australian and called suitcases 'ports' and said 'beg yours' for 'beg your pardon' which amused us greatly. She was an orphan and a person cast upon the waters of life with no context or relations. She was terribly religious, probably over-religious and it could have been this that influenced the nuns in this order to keep her outside the congregation. She earned her keep by being a hard worker and domestic assistant and toiled tirelessly. The Sisters of the Good Shepherd seemed to me a sensible bunch without that primitive Irish element which could sometimes be found in the congregation of the Sisters of Mercy.

The Mother Superior was called Mother John Udes and her assistant was called nothing else but 'Big Mother' as she was rather large. I never knew her real name. These two women thought that Phyllis should experience 'family life' and asked my mother if she could spend time in our family. Clearly they had no idea that they were committing poor Phyllis to 'Family life' outside the usual benevolent parameters. In short Phyllis was sent to the 'lion's den' to sink or swim. My father had no time for Phyllis and poor Phyllis had never in her life rubbed shoulders with many men probably only priests let alone such an incendiary personality such as my father but to give her due she stayed often and coped. She was privy to shouting matches, swearing, most of which she had never heard before, but which must have shaken her soul to its roots and domestic turmoil not seen in the bosom of 'Big Mother' and Mother John Udes. Her way of coping was to laugh a lot and talk a lot which drove my father insane. My mother's critical faculties had been cauterised long ago and she accepted anyone into her bosom as long as they went to Mass, confession, said their morning prayers and believed in the infallibility of the Pope. Phyllis ticked all these boxes.

When it was announced that Phyllis was coming to visit there would always be a collective groan rippling through the household. Someone had to vacate a bed and someone else had to share a bedroom with her. My father would rail loudly but my mother would be obdurate and could not be swayed. The tour-de-force of my mother's determination to slot Phyllis into our lives was when she suddenly announced that she had invited Phyllis to drive to Auckland for my brother Dermot's profession as a Marist Brother. My father went into a rage of such ferocity that I am sure the Hills next door might have been tempted to call the police. I cannot blame my father at all but to Auckland they went and as my father had predicted Phyllis yapped during the entire journey. There were many stops to make a visit in any passing Catholic church and, if not a visit, the sign of the cross was mandatory as one drove by.

Chapter 13 – The Hard Bit

Dear Amelia and Fionn:

When I was fifteen my mother had a complete mental collapse. There had been many dress rehearsals after the birth of many of her children, but this was the big one. She entered a tormented phase which caused her great suffering and from which she only got relief after two leucotomies in 1970 and 1971. My father was beside himself for despite everything he was fond of my mother and showed it constantly by hugging and kissing her. She was not demonstrative at all but he had given up on reciprocation many years ago. This mental breakdown took the form of obsessions often with sexual overtones laced with overwhelming guilt.

I had spent my first year at St Mary's and had sat school certificate and was at home for the holidays. I had managed to get a job in Milne and Choyce department store for the holidays in the china department. When I announced this to the family there was a cacophony of derision from the perches and of course the expected cry of 'a bull in a china shop' as I was quite gangly and moved with a loose-limbed awkwardness and was often being told not to 'barge' so not an ideal candidate for a china department of a department store. Their cries made me quite unconsciously determined not to break a thing and not a thing did I break while all around me the other temporary school holiday workers broke crystal vases, cracked glasses and dropped cups . With my first pay I bought my parents a stainless steel cutlery set for Christmas. Stainless steel had become popular for tableware. They received this without much enthusiasm or even interest and the bone handled set was removed and stored away somewhere. They continued to use this set until their final days in Palmerston North.

My sister Margaret had done a similarly generous thing when she first started working and with one of her early pay-packets had bought a pair of red pointy toed shoes for me. I can see these shoes today. I absolutely loved them. They were the absolute height of footwear fashion. They were boldly red and I wore them all the time outside school hours. When I was at home my mother would follow me around the house telling me about her worries which were bottomless and always on the same theme. No reply of reassurance changed anything. 'I'm worried Susie' she would say. 'what are you worried about Mum?' I would reply endlessly, then listen while a catalogue of absolutely nonsensical anxieties poured out. They always centred around what she had said to someone who would then think this, that or the next thing. Or she needed to wash all her clothes as she went to the toilet and she thought something had got contaminated. Worst of all she would say she had had impure thoughts and needed to get to confession immediately.

I never enquired as to what these thoughts were about, but she was willing to volunteer and would say she had had impure thoughts about a priest and in particular Archbishop McKeefry. I tried to be the one listening to this stuff so as to diffuse the powder keg of my father's reaction if she poured out this stuff to him. It was depressing and went on and on and on every day and all day. My School Certificate results plopped into the letterbox but it seemed pointless to tell anyone that I had scraped a Pass so I kept it to myself, although I was rather relieved. I had failed music for two reasons. Hopeless teaching and an earthquake mid exam in a brick building.

My mother already had an obsession with needles and she had read once that someone had sat on a needle which had entered the blood stream and taken a quick trip to the heart and killed the person. If anyone lost a needle in our house no one could rest until it was found. Once someone lost a needle on a bed. My mother was convinced that the needle had penetrated the mattress and she would not rest until that mattress had been discarded completely which was not done lightly but such was her distress that it was done. As the holidays progressed she got worse and worse. The family doctor was at a loss so the big guns were brought in, in the form of my uncle who was a doctor and surgeon referred to already in this narrative. He had connections in other areas of the medical profession which would have helped.

She was sent to Piketeora Mental Hospital in Wellington. This was a private hospital so money whose source is unknown to me was shelled out. Uncle Ro was able to keep a close watch on her during this time and his influence may have helped in some ways but her condition was not helped in any way. This went on for much of my sixth form year but details are scarce as we were not told anything so gnawing anxiety as to her state of being prevailed. During my last year in the 6th form nothing had changed or improved so it was decided to put her into the mental hospital in Porirua. This was the dreaded last resort as Porirua was fondly called the 'loony bin' and people who went there were in our minds beyond redemption and had lost all hope and were literally lunatics. My mother was there for two years.

I had to hurriedly leave school as it appeared that I was the obvious choice for the job of running the house and attending to the other three children as I was at a point of change in my life. School had finished for me and the next phase was ready to begin. So at the age of 17 I returned to Palmerston North to become a housekeeper. I had wanted to go back and do the 7th form but this was not to be. I was hurriedly and possibly undeservedly accredited with University Entrance and once that was done I left before school broke up. I left my friends and returned to a city where I had no friends except Helen Morpeth. The next year was grim.

My father was in deep grief as the problem of my mother's mental condition appeared insoluble. We children crept around in a state of abject misery coupled with fear at his regular outbursts. He would frequently go down to the front room, shut the door and howl uncontrollably. I could not find it in my heart to feel sorry for him as he made our lives doubly difficult. I was in charge of all the cooking, cleaning, washing and generally making sure the 'three little ones' were kept clean, dressed properly, cleaned their teeth and did their homework especially their Catechism. It was horrible for them as they were young and sad. We all missed our mother and dreaded what would become of her for, as usual, information was almost zero. I do not think even my father was told anything. I know she hardly ever saw a doctor and dread to think what life was like for her receiving regular bouts of shock treatment and being in this dreadful place with no prospect of ever getting better, being tormented by her mind and never able to come home.

We went to visit her from time to time. Porirua Hospital was the most joyless grim place I have ever been into. My mother would appear gaunt, haunted and hollow eyed. She looked a picture of misery and to see our mother whom we all loved dearly looking like that was quite unbearable. We would then return home to carry on our lives having no idea what the outcome would be and when this would all end and normality return. It never did. Once we were allowed to bring her home for two days. She crept around the house hardly speaking and if she did the subject matter was the same as ever a convoluted and circular litany of senseless stories of how she had done the wrong thing and what terrible thoughts she was having. Her eyes would stare without seeing and had no spark of life in them at all. She was terrified of hell and was convinced that that was where she was going.

Years later when I asked her where she was going when she died, she lifted her thumb and pointed it downwards towards the ground and said 'down there'. Once after one of the visits home we were returning her to the hospital. As we turned off the main road to go towards the hospital, she opened the car door and attempted to leap out. We all screamed and I leaned forward from the back seat and grabbed her. 'Don't take me back there' she said 'I can't go back there'. My mother was never given to outbursts of any kind. She never shouted and was never ever theatrical so for her to do this showed the level of desperation she felt. For her we were returning her to a place of torture. A nurse came out unlocking several doors with a huge bunch of keys on her belt and led her back like a lamb to the slaughter. We all stared as she was led away feeling numb with grief and drove back to Palmerston North in dumb silence.

And so our lives went on superimposed by a pall of unhappiness. When I look back I feel such sympathy for the three youngest children. I was seventeen old enough to manage emotionally but they were 13, 11 and 9. They needed and wanted their mother and I was certainly no substitute. Coupled with that was an angry unhappy and desperate father who was incapable of reaching out to them with some sort of comforting hand. My father was I know a passionate person. He never understood his own feelings. They were just raw feelings with absolutely no analysis, so we were all high and dry, seen and certainly not heard. I do not think those three children have ever fully recovered from this loss at this time of their lives. It was a time when nothing was said. No explanations given and therefore an absence of hope. I know it was not death but at the time it certainly felt like a permanent absence almost like death.

I had absolutely no money, no clothes, no shoes and no way of obtaining any. Having been at boarding school there was not much need for ordinary clothes as a uniform was worn most of the time but once I left school I needed clothes. My father kept a tight rein on the purse strings and never gave us anything. He did all the shopping and was careful with money as he had to be. I remember that I did not even have enough money to buy sanitary pads. I once bravely asked him if he could give me the money to buy my brother Joseph a school shirt as his were threadbare. There was an outraged reaction to this and Joseph continued to wear threadbare shirts. Finally in the second part of the year it was decided that Lucy would go to boarding school at St Mary's in Wellington. By this time she was twelve. My sister Philippa was a nun there so it was thought that she could keep a eye on Lucy, which she did. Rolly was sent to the Marist Brother's Novitiate in Tuakau. I have no idea whether he had expressed a desire to become a Marist Brother. My brother Dermot had attended this establishment and had become a Marist Brother which he is to this day.

That left me at home with my brother Joseph. This eased the domestic burden and things went on as before with no sign of recovery for my mother. I decided to try to get a job in the Palmerston North Public Library as I was desperate to have at least some money. I succeeded in doing this and this was the beginning of a long and satisfying career in this profession and of course I was following the suggestion of my kind cousin Dorothy who had suggested it to me a few years earlier. Dorothy had asked me when I was about fifteen if I had any idea as to what I would do when I left school. I did not of course and knew the limitations of my options. She said 'why don't you become a librarian?' I agreed that this would be a good option but, to be honest, if she had suggested that I become an airline pilot I would have agreed to that such was my trust in her.

I loved this job, and in the Palmerston North Library I was quickly promoted from dog's body at the desk and returned books shelving to being put in charge of the ordering process. It was not my job to choose the books but to order what Miss Green the Deputy City Librarian had chosen. She was a kind warm amiable person with whom I worked well. When I eventually left she gave me a glowing reference which stood me

in good stead for my next job sometime later at the Wellington Public
Library. The staff were all nice. I especially remember Mrs Grover. She
was kind and motherly which was nice for me. They all knew that my
situation was 'difficult' at home and although it wasn't mentioned I felt
their kindliness. Then there was the student help Michael Martin a gangly
good-natured boy who came in part time. He spent endless years at
University failing as in those days the government paid all the fees so the
fiscal motivation pressure was missing.

The music librarian was Mrs Morrison. Her son was that very
talented photographer Robin Morrison who died very young. I remember
him as a schoolboy coming to visit his mother in the library. At this time
I was a still in the practising Catholic harness and it was clear what Mrs
Morrison thought of my benighted beliefs as I trotted out my
programmed response to any questions I was asked. Once I announced
that it was a 'Holy day of Obligation' and that I had to go to Mass. Mrs
Morrison snorted with derision as I would too today. Then there was
Lorna, a large lumbering person who never got far as she was terribly
lazy but good with the public to whom she would chat for hours while the
rest of us did the hard yards. The city librarian was Mr Trudgeon who
was quite remote but nice enough. At this time men were usually in
charge of Public Libraries although I am sure there were exceptions.

In Wellington I encountered the kind and dignified Mr Perry. These
men at the top had little to do with the daily nuts and bolts of the running
of the library but presided more over the fiscal management and were
answerable to the city council for their prudent financial stewardship. Fay
Jewell ran the children's department. She was bustling and efficient.
Unfortunately I had had a bad experience of this when I was about eight
years old. I had gone to the library to take some books back and get some
more. There I had seen a school friend and was chatting amiably when
Miss Jewell came up and castigated me angrily for 'talking in the library'.
I was absolutely mortified and upset as I was so nervously law abiding at
this time of my life. As a result I never went back to the library because I
was scared of Miss Jewell. This was a great loss as we did not have books
at home except religious ones such as 'The Lives of the Saints' and 'Saint
Theresa of Avila' and 'Therese of Lisieux', also known as the 'Little
flower', and 'Pencilling Prisoner' the experiences in captivity of an

Australian catholic priest in Korea. He 'pencilled' his experiences of clinging to his faith against great odds. I had read all these books multiple times and was hungry for things to read.

I resorted to the National Geographic magazine which my father subscribed to which came once a month. From reading these I gained some insight into the fact that there was a large and fascinating world outside the geographical boundaries of Palmerston North and made an unconscious decision to go and explore when I grew up. My sister Pauline read a lot and would bring books home from the library which I read sometimes. My mother also read to us quite a lot when we were in bed. Books such as the 'Faraway Tree' series by Enid Blyton and 'The Seven Little Australians' by Ethel Turner. Later we seemed to acquire the 'Famous Five' books which I read voraciously, but the public library remained out of bounds. When I finally worked with Fay Jewell I would look at her and think 'If you only knew what an influence you had on me'. It certainly was more of a testament to my timidity rather than her brief act of annoyance and I certainly did not blame her at all.

During this time however my mother remained absent and there were many domestic crises which upset me a great deal. When this happened I always turned to my sister MaryClare and her husband Lou. Long distant calls in those days were called toll calls and cost money and we were simply not allowed to make them. The only way I could talk to them and get some comfort was to ring and get them to ring back as my father would have spied the call on the phone bill and been annoyed at this unnecessary expense. This is what I did and made many distraught calls to them. They were wonderful and it was this connection that helped me to get through. Lou would say 'We are coming to get you'. I would never have allowed this to happen as the situation was not dire enough for that and I could not abandon my poor brother Joseph. But they were a safety valve for me and a great comfort. Eventually however, a 'straw did break the camel's back'. I overcooked the cauliflower and it fell to bits. My father lost all control and I had to run from the house and down the road as I actually feared for my safety. I ran to Spelman's verandah and crouched there quivering with fear. I had to abandon Joseph who no doubt was cowering somewhere. I stayed there for ages.

There had been another occasion when I had felt that fear. We had gone a holiday to Turangi to stay at my Uncle Con's bach. My mother was in a dark place so it was a very forlorn group who set forth on this excursion. The bach was set in the bush so it was a bit dismal anyway. My mother started on her catalogue of 'worries' and my father lost control. Something else set him off as well as that. It was probably the thought of a week here with him solely in charge. Suddenly he started shouting and picked up a carving knife and headed towards the little knot of children huddled near the door. He advanced menacingly towards us. We all screamed in unison and ran very fast out the back door and into the bush. If I am honest I don't actually think he would ever have harmed us but when his helpless frustrations boiled right over there was definitely a threat.

My father was not fundamentally violent despite some incidents which might indicate that he was. He would sometimes take off the belt from his pants and lash out but by the time he had got it through the loops the person to be lashed was far away. After a long wait in the bush, crouched together, we crept tentatively towards the house. I already knew that my father's rages were like extreme weather. They reached a high point then slowly petered out. Like a storm one had to sit them out. This holiday was terrible.

We went to Sunday to Mass at this tiny church the size of a small garage. There was a handful of people there and we were all sitting close to one another. As Communion approached my mother clutched me and said in a loud stage whisper 'Susie, I'm not worthy to receive the body and blood of Christ'. Heads turned and even the priest flinched. I whispered back through gritted teeth. 'You are Mum' but she repeated this several times and our mortification knew no bounds. Eventually she went up to the altar and received communion. I waited with dread that she might spit it out, but she would never have done that because that would have been a dreadful sin to defile the scared host in any shape or form. As we left the church people stared as though their eyes would pop out as we scuttled hastily to the safety of the car.

Eventually I did leave Spelman's porch and crept home. Once again an uneasy peace had descended. That night I went to bed but could not sleep. Around 5am I got up, got dressed collected a few things and rode around to Helen Morpeth's house. I tapped on her bedroom window. She pulled the curtain across and looking surprised opened the window and I climbed in. I explained to her that I could not stay at home as it had become an impossible situation. 'You can stay here' she said as I knew she would. The next morning some hasty explanations had to be given to her mother. She was understanding as she could see that I was a great deal rattled. She was not happy with the situation but was willing to help out. She must have rung my father to tell him where I was. I felt terrible abandoning Joseph but by this time I knew that I could not take any more and had to remove myself.

I felt guilty about Joseph that I would sometimes meet him on the corner of Carroll Street and Featherston Street to hear his catechism and generally question him as to his wellbeing. How would I ever know but I accepted his reassuring answers at face value. As the end of the second year of my mother's incarceration loomed, it was decided something better had to be done for Joseph and it was decided that he should go and live with my Aunt Cassie and Uncle Barry in Wellington. Their youngest child Mark was around his age and he could go to school with him. And so it happened. 'One more won't make any difference' my aunt said and Joseph slotted well into their household. This 'straw did not break this camel's back' because this camel's back was incredibly strong. My mother came home but she was still far from well. In fact she was just as bad as ever but there was absolutely no progress being made at Porirua Hospital so it was felt that with no onerous domestic burdens she might as well be at home.

After this, with no children left at home, I decided to shift to Wellington. I was so eager to remove myself from Palmerston North that wild horses could not keep me there. I had never liked this city and once I departed I knew that I would never return. And return I did not. A child growing up somewhere has no context upon which to base any reflections on this place. It is only later when new experiences and places overlay this first domicile strong realisations come to the fore. For me it is the sea which means more to me than anything and to be near it is paramount, but this realisation took many years to discover and be realised. Fortunately I am now in constant proximity and, better still, often in it feeling its delicious embrace in Summer when daily plunges are the norm. As a child we sometimes visited my Aunt and Uncle in Hataitai in Wellington. Their house looked right over the sea with such an immediate view that would transfix me for hours. It made me feel happy and calm but I was still too young to be conscious how much it meant to me and still too young to think and plan to eventually live near the sea.

Chapter 14 – And So I Moved to Wellington

Dear Amelia and Fionn:

I got a job in the Wellington Public Library, in the Reference Department, and once again I had landed in a happy place surrounded by and large by people I got to know and liked very much. We had a lot of fun and going to work was anticipated with pleasure. The best part of this job was the shift work so working at night until the library closed at 9pm was part of the regime. This meant mornings were often free for chores or lazing about. It was during this time that I decided to embark on studying for my Library Certificate as it was possible to do this part time which suited me perfectly. I had not been to university at this stage as any plans I might have had in that sphere were stymied by the domestic needs in Palmerston North. I felt I needed qualifications of some sort and felt an urge to start the ball rolling and this seemed to be a logical first step

At first I was flatting in Rolleston Street with my sister Pauline and as already recounted my sister in law to be Pauline Gardiner. However, once I established myself at the library, an opportunity arose for a place in a flat in Coolidge Street in Brooklyn. This street was off Washington Avenue and had a lovely sea view. I had met Margaret Cavell in the library where she worked in the Children's Department. We got our heads together and decided to find a flat which we did. Margaret was wonderful. She was small, energetic, motivated and efficient. She was neat and tidy and loved routines so our flat ran like clockwork and we always had a roster for the chores which meant that the flat was always orderly and clean. This suited me fine. Margaret was a competent sewer and could 'run something up' in a trice with very little effort. Margaret and I shared a room and we found another flatmate for the other room. Her name was Alison Lee and she was a nurse.

Alison was a very talented person and was amazing at needlework. She would make incredible tablecloths and could make any garment you could name and I watched in awe such were my deficiencies in this area. Alison was a solemn person not given to levity at all but that is not to say she was humourless, as she was not, But she was one of the most capable people I had ever met. She could make any silk purse out of any sow's ear. I was rather like my mother in matters of domestic prowess but I did not mind as other people seemed to fill any gaps which became pressing. I was neither a gardener nor seamstress. Alison left to travel and later I would flat with her in South London in an appalling bedsit in Stockwell. We later moved to the more salubrious area in Muswell Hill. By then she had met Richard whom she subsequently married and who was a talented jeweller. Alison died young of breast cancer leaving Richard and two young boys.

After Alison left a law student called Anne Clancy moved in. She would use such hallowed terms as Equity and Torts, words which for me were shrouded in mystery but would later also trip off my tongue. But I had no idea about that then. She started seeing a fellow law student called Ken Hingston who would later become a Maori Land Court Judge and by whom she got pregnant. The latter flew to the hills, or maybe hid under the bench, but there were no equitable remedies for Anne and she was left to fend alone. Her parents were horrified as they came from Greymouth and were devout Catholics. She stayed in our flat and continued going to Law School for as long as she could. She absolutely loved the Law and was an excellent student.

Towards the end, my sister MaryClare and her husband Lou took her in and she stayed there until the baby was born. They had a small house and three young children so this was an act of true goodness. Afterwards the child, called Juliette, was sent down to Greymouth to be brought up by Anne's parents. They had had three children of their own so I am sure that this was the last thing they wanted. How they explained the child I do not know but I was privy to the moment when Anne handed over the baby to her parents at a bus stop and I will never forget that as long as I live. I saw Anne's distress and witnessed her anguish at that moment. Babies did not mean a great deal to me then as I had seen rather too many of them but later when you were born Amelia I reflected on these events and only then did I appreciate the depth of Anne's pain.

By now I had purchased a Lambretta motor scooter which I called Hildegard. I have no idea why I chose such a name but a few years later when I was au pairing in Germany the mother of the household was called Hildegard so maybe my unconscious was fast forwarding. Later

131

too I became aware of Hildegard of Bingen who was alive in the 11th century and was a mystic among other things. I had never heard of her when I called my scooter Hildegard. In those days crash helmets were not mandatory so Margaret and I would set off each morning on Hildegard dressed in our smart work clothes to start our day's work in the library. I would often drive up to my sister MaryClare's house in Wentworth Street which was close by. There I would spend time with my three nieces and nephews Anne, Bede and Catherine.

I grew very fond of these children and they of me as we spent a lot of time together when they were small and impressionable. My nephew Bede recounted how he loved to hear the putt putt of my scooter as I approached and would shout 'Susie's coming'. Their household had a big influence on me as my sister MaryClare and her husband Lou could not have departed more from their own respective childhood domestic patterns. They had contemporary art on the walls, beautiful pottery dotted around and MaryClare's cooking bore no relation to the culinary outpourings of my mother. She made exotic dishes such as Nasi goreng, using rice in the way the Malaysian students had, and other dishes where the pattern of meat and two vegetables was seldom the blueprint.

As one walked though their front door there was a beautiful Chagall print called 'Woman on a Horse'. The woman's dress is placed below her breasts and her right arm is flung above her head, while the man sitting on the horse with her is tightly clutching her waist. A visitor to the house loosely allied to the family made the immortal utterance as he came through the door. 'She's got TB'. 'TB?' was the puzzled rejoinder. 'Yes' he replied 'TB.' Pause .. 'two beauts'. Of course he was promptly consigned to the dustbin of ignorance and possibly never darkened the door again, I know not. I do know that I learned a lot from being a regular visitor to their house.

Hildegard my scooter, played a role in a more sinister experience I must digress at this stage to recount as it was very frightening. I sometimes rode my scooter from Wellington to Palmerston North to dutifully visit my parents. I would leave after work on Friday and would arrive after dark. I was hurtling along the Foxton Straight. It was dark and there was absolutely no traffic when a man on a high-powered motorbike came up beside me. 'Where are you heading?' he said. I replied that I was going to visit my parents in Palmerston North. He proceeded to ask further questions which in those days I was programmed to answer politely. After a while he whizzed off but before long he stopped and waited for me to catch up which eventually I did. It was starting to feel like a 'come and see my birds' moment and I was anxiously looking out for a house I could escape into but it was pitch black and nothing seemed viable. He continued to slowly ride beside me.

After a while he roared off into the night but continued to do this cat and mouse thing until finally for some reason which I know not he disappeared permanently into the night. I started to have a nervous reaction to this and was very glad to see the lights of Palmerston North and to this day have no idea if he had evil intentions but decided not act upon them. At this point in my life I could not thank the St Philomena cord or the miraculous medal or the scapular as I had discarded these protective adjuncts a long time ago. I drove up the drive at 35 Beresford Street shaking quite a lot. My father came roaring out like a madman saying 'Get that junk off the driveway'. I was so alarmed that I drove straight into the closed garage door cracking the wood and damaging it. To give my father his due he calmed down as he probably saw that he had brought about this nervous reaction and my face possibly wore the marks of my earlier shock. I did not mention my Foxton Straight experience to my parents but pondered upon it for a long time afterwards and never drove Hildegard to Palmerston North again. Newman's bus seemed the safer option.

Later when my mother was a patient in Porirua Mental Hospital I would pack up a picnic and proceed on the trusty Hildegard to try to ease her misery by taking her out. She would emerge from the portals of that terrible place looking haunted and defeated and climb meekly on the back of my scooter. We would then proceed to some leafy glade which I had earlier scoped out. I would spread a picnic rug and try to entice her to eat. She was like a wraith and still full of tormenting obsessions. I remember one in particular involved another patient called Bridie. It was the same revolving door of 'I said this and she would think this.' There was no gainsaying as any counterarguments I would proffer were as 'idle as a painted ship upon a painted ocean'. We would climb back onto Hildegard and I would return her to the hospital with a heart as heavy as a heart can be without doing some irreparable damage to it. My mother would re-enter the hospital as though she was going to her own execution. I wondered what lay behind those walls as we were not allowed beyond a certain point. I knew that she had regular visits from my sister MaryClare who at the time had three very young children who she would pile into her small car and head out to Porirua. My Aunty Cassie also went to see her. She also had a busy demanding life but out she would faithfully trot every two weeks. My sister Pauline who was studying at Victoria University went out too, but all the visitors in the world could not assuage the anguish and hopelessness my mother and all of us felt as absolutely no progress seemed to be being made and doctor's visits seemed to be a rare event probably culminating in another round of shock treatment.

During this time in Wellington my sister Margaret who lived in Sydney announced that she was getting married. My mother was too unwell to attend which meant that no one would be there, so I decided to go. It would be an adventure. I told Margaret who immediately asked me to be her bridesmaid. This made me happy as I had never been a bridesmaid before and have never since. It was decided that I would bring my own dress and shoes which Margaret would trust me to choose. In I went to Thomson's silks in Willis Street which was the smartest dress material shop in Wellington. I took my trusty friend Margaret Cavell as she had a good eye for these things and after much humming and hawing and many visits in our lunch break from the library we settled on a turquoise Thai silk fabric. The person who served us was always helpful and was privy to our many visits as he helped us make a choice. When we finally alighted on the material we wanted he was very pleased and uttered the immortal words 'Madam this material will suit you very well and make up real smart at your sister's wedding'. 'Real smart' has gone down in the annals as, being a seasoned stickler for grammar, I knew that that construction was not right.

If I had learnt nothing else in my years at school, I had learnt English grammar. So off I went to Sydney armed with my dress and high heeled shoes. Margaret's friends were kind to me especially the best man called Ken and I had a good time and I am sure I 'made up real smart'. I had my hair done and my nails manicured which for me was a treat. Margaret had earlier in Palmerston North been presented as a debutante.

134

This involved having a long white dress made which had to pass muster for modesty as the debutantes were presented to the Bishop, and he must not be tempted. There was female debutante overseer whose job it was to check all the dresses beforehand to ensure they were suitable. It transpired that Margaret's dress, which she probably made herself did not as there was a hint of cleavage and the bishop would have had to practice 'custody of the eyes' as she curtsied before him. A solution was found in the form of two lace handkerchiefs placed judiciously where the cleavage threatened and the matter was solved to everyone's satisfaction. The tour de force of Debutante balls was the one at government house where the debs were presented to the Governor General. Those chosen for this had to have societal credentials of a high order and dwell on the top branches of the social tree. It did not occur to me to be presented. I was probably thinking at some unconscious level that one had to be presentable to be presented.

During my time in Wellington I also decided to have another go at getting my driver's licence. I had already embarked on this process in Palmerston North but my instructor was impatient and unfriendly which did not result in an enthusiastic response to his instructions. In fact, it made me more nervous than I already was and culminated in a near miss with a large plate-glass window at the back of Milne and Choyce when I put my foot on the accelerator instead of the brake and only through the good fortune of a dual control car was a disaster averted. The instructor turned to me and said 'I do not want to teach you any more'. The feeling was mutual so he dropped me off never to be seen again.

In Wellington I thought I would try again and enrolled with the Willis Street School of Driving. My teacher was a confident and rather brash English person called Brian Foy. I made more progress with him but there was another more sinister side to him which came to the fore one day during a lesson. 'My flat is just up here' he said, 'Would you like to come up for a cup of coffee?' Call me naive because that is just what I was so up I went. Once there he pretended to bustle around putting on the jug and preparing the cups. Suddenly he grabbed my hand and led me towards his bedroom. 'Take off your clothes' he said. I stared in disbelief when suddenly the door opened and his flatmate came in. 'Stop that Brian' he said. From that it was clear that this was not the first time for the dubious Brian Foy. I walked out and left his house. After that a different instructor came and picked me up from the library for a driving lesson and eventually I passed my test and became a licenced driver. I did not report this incident and it says something of those times that it did not occur to me to do so, and it was lucky that the flatmate intervened. I am unable to report whether or not I had my scapula, miraculous medal and Philomena cord on but I think by then I had discarded such adornments.

I also auditioned for Opera Technique's production of John Gay's The Beggar's Opera and to my surprise got a part in the chorus as Mrs. Coaxer, a woman of doubtful virtue. This was produced by Dick Johnstone and Patrick Flynn was the musical director. After all my theatrical exploits with Helen Morpeth I had gained a taste for the theatre but alas my talent was not of a high order, but I had a lot of fun. Patrick Flynn was rather bad-tempered and I was slightly scared of him. He would pick on certain people such as Bobby Bell who was also in the St Mary of the Angel's choir and also picked on by Maxwell Fernie from time to time. I must have put on my stricken look as he never picked on me. This time a cleavage was required and I did not have one so a contraption had to be employed to push up my bosom and give me one. After all I was a prostitute and having fulsome bosoms was a given. At the end of the season there was a Beggar's Ball to which I went in the company of Tony Donovan, not exactly an Adonis but served the purpose at the time. MaryClare and Lou came as did Pauline with Roy Murphy, and Pauline Gardiner with my brother Tony. We dressed up appropriately and all looked rather good I thought.

My duties in the Reference Department were at the beginning behind the desk, helping with enquiries and shelving books. But quite soon I was put in charge of doing the inter-library loans. This was quite rewarding and sometimes challenging as in pre-internet days all communications were done by mail and telephone. People often asked for obscure items which required a considerable amount of detective work, which I enjoyed. The person in charge of us was Anne Rewiti, a quiet dignified person who treated us with kindness and respect. The next person in the pecking order was Win Kayes. After that in the hierarchy was Mr Silver who proved to be my nemesis, which I will relate in due course. Next in the pecking order was a remote taciturn man called Brian

Keen. He always dressed impeccably but never engaged in conversation with the staff.

At the top was Mr Perry whose attributes I have already described. At that level we called people Miss Kayes and discarded the Christian name. They called us by our Christian names. Win Kayes was shy and nervous and found it hard to deal with difficult patrons who cropped up from time to time. Libraries, as we all know, can be places where the lonely and disjointed congregate sometimes just to be warm and often just to be amongst people. There was one man who came in every day. He would sit at a table and read magazines and sometimes books. From time-to-time he would pick up his newspaper and start crashing and banging the table, the library shelves and anything else which was in his path. Win Kayes was terrified of this man and she always sent me to deal with him. I was not in the slightest bit scared as I could tell that he was fundamentally harmless. I would speak calmly to him and eventually he would stop. He never struck any people when in this state. Today we might call it a form of Turettes but then we had no definitions for it. I knew that he was not menacing as he had a kind face and soft eyes, but he just couldn't help himself when the urge took him to lash out.

The fun I had was mostly centred around Helen Burbery. Helen was larger than life, incredibly positive and never ever uttered an unkind word against anyone. When we met we were slightly suspicious of one another. She of me as she suspected a raging socialist waiting to break out and I of her as I suspected a raging Tory lying quite peacefully within her. She had attended a private school called Chilton St James which I, in my intolerance, thought could never produce anyone with liberal tendencies. The hallmark of such people was a triangular scarf around their heads and knotted not under their chin but **on** their chin. The scarves were always paisley. Helen always wore her scarf like this. Her nickname from school was Bubbles Burbery. This was another sign of a private school product as they often had nicknames which often highlighted a character trait and Helen was definitely bubbly.

I was also to discover Helen was the least political person I had ever met. She was neither one thing nor the other and embraced the whole human race within her ample form and when she was with one her full attention was given. Once Helen and I had let our various guards down we became the best of friends. With Helen it was a crowded field as everyone was her friend, but I managed to insinuate myself into her inner circle and eventually met her family in Auckland who like Helen were generous and enthusiastic. Helen loved jazz and played quite competently by ear. There was a piano down in the basement in the library where Helen and I would disappear to at our morning and afternoon tea breaks and play, sing and dance. We often did this in work time too but no one ever took us to task. It was just accepted that Miss Dowling and Miss Burbery did this in the stack room.

The person in charge of the stack room, which was where all the non-current library material was kept, was called Ralph Herne. He was quite a young and rather dour, taciturn English person who fully accepted our impromptu concerts. In fact I know he did like it and never tried to dampen our enthusiasm. How could anyone gainsay Helen whose booming posh voice simply announced to him that we would just be doing a few numbers before returning to the sober environments from whence we came namely the Reference Room and the Commercial Rooms respectively. We both played the piano and sometimes we blasted out impromptu duets which we made up as we went along.

The library clients loved Helen and would often ask specifically for her to answer their requests in the Commercial Room. She would fix them with her full interested gaze, always remembered their names and what they were interested in and always pretended that she knew exactly what they were talking about. The subject material in the Commercial room was not exactly riveting but Helen acted as though the composition of epoxy resins was just the thing which was occupying her mind and set about steering them in the right direction. The other staff in the Commercial room were also interesting people. Michael Wooliscroft was in charge. He was another enthusiast for life and despite the fact that he had a wife and two small children was always inviting us around for parties and dinners and seemed to have unlimited energy. His wife Elaine always entered into any gatherings we had with gusto. Of course we had no idea what having two small children was like and accepted it as our right to be entertained by them. I still have the 21st birthday present they gave me which is a brass gong used for summoning people to meals or an impending tsunami.

Michael later became the head librarian at the University of Otago. He was clever and accomplished and faced any task with unbounded confidence and energy. He could cut to the chase with any task he undertook. He was tall and good-looking and we were all fond of him. Then there was Adrienne Yska, another member of the Commercial Room staff. Adrian was great fun and also very sought after by the Commercial department patrons. She was hardworking and energetic and always focussed in her communications with another person. I often wonder if the citizens of Wellington had any idea what a taonga that library was and what great people worked there. Of course I believe that the quality of any organisation is defined by the quality of the top layers and Mr Perry the city librarian was a good, civilised human being. He treated everyone with respect no matter how lowly their task in the library was. He was very good to me in two incidents which I will recount in the fullness of time.

My friend and flatmate, Margaret Cavell, worked in the children's department. The librarian in charge was Alison Grant who was an efficient and down-to-earth person. Margaret was a great bonus to that department due to the qualities outlined above. She dealt with the school groups firmly and efficiently as they poured into the library at regular intervals. One such school group was led by a teacher called Ramon Parbhu and Margaret eventually married him. Ramon also became the principal of Berhamphore Primary School. Another person who worked in the children's department was Mrs Bottlander. To this day and to my shame I do not know where she came from. At that point in my life I had little or no curiosity as to how such a person as Mrs Bottlander had landed in New Zealand and she never spoke of her past. I am absolutely sure she had fled the war and was possibly Jewish.

The input of information into our lives was absolutely minimal. The *Manawatu Evening Standard* came into the house and as already mentioned the *National Geographic*, but apart from that only religious tracts were available. As a result we knew a great deal about the missionaries in the Far East or the orphans of some African country but absolutely nothing else. We did not listen to the radio and had no television when I was a child. As a result the experiences of the likes of Mrs Bottlander and her history were absolutely unknown to us. Although

I was born in October 1945 and Hitler had only been dead for six months the war had hardly touched us and we knew almost nothing about it. My Uncle Ro had served in his capacity as a medical person but my father had not gone due to the fact that he had lots of children. I have been told too that it's because he had flat feet but that has not been verified and I am sure the main reason he was not called up was because he had skills and experience much needed at home.

So I had no questions to ask Mrs Bottlander as I knew nothing about the recent history of the world. She was a great character and an absolute chain smoker. In those days smoking was allowed at one's place of work which is hard to believe today. She had an appalling cough which bespoke lung damage which probably carried her off. I never heard anything more of her after I left the library but I am reminded of her often as I still have the beautiful green ginger jar which she gave me for my 21st birthday. She probably had it already and passed it on to me for the occasion. I was once told by someone who saw it that it could be valuable but I have never tried to find out. Unfortunately I dropped and broke the lid which I still have in many pieces.

There was another person who had fled worn torn Europe called Mrs Vartik. Her full name was Vartike de Varte. She ran the New Zealand room and there was nothing she did not know about the contents of this department. People would come asking all sorts of complex questions, trying to track down material from government sources. She was eternally helpful, knowledgeable and pleasant but again I have no idea what her story was but it was probably again a story of an escape from oppression and possibly death.

Behind the reference room on the 1st floor two pen pushers worked. One was Mr Cross, another chain smoker, and a Mr Gray. What they did was a mystery to me but Mr Cross was an insignificant little man who took it upon himself to disparage Mrs Vartik. Of course he wasn't worthy to let her name pass his lips, such was his mediocrity. In those days my feelings and opinions were in their infancy but I knew instinctively that the genesis of his criticism was that she was a foreigner who had a strong foreign accent and 'what was she doing in this country?'. Now I would see it with the clarity of age and deliver a riposte to him which would silence him forever. Then my experience of life was so limited and the certainty of my opinions so much in its infancy that I remained silent and probably just shrugged but I have remembered his remarks and they make my blood boil even to this day when I give them mental attention.

The person in charge of the Reference Department was a Mr Silver. He was amiable enough but as to efficiency I have my doubts. Anne Rewiti did the hard yards and he seemed to swan about doing not much at all. He had an eye for an attractive female and set his sights on such a one called Ursula Utting. She was a university student and worked part time. She had soft blond hair, beautiful skin and warm blue eyes and an amiable disposition. Mr Silver could not keep his roving brown eyes off her. He was sensible enough to keep it at that, but it was clear that he favoured her above the rest of us. Then there was Mr Wright. He was a complete drip which would have been okay if he also did not have a PhD in laziness. The library patrons avoided him completely, so he got away with doing almost no work. He had the job as some relation was high up in the council and had advocated with Mr Perry.

One Christmas we played a terrible trick on him in which I am ashamed to say I was a leading player. We managed by stealth and sleight of hand to attach two pieces of holly onto his shoulder blades. He had no idea and walked around for some time with these encumbrances. We watched as the patrons stifled their laughter and were rather unbridled in ours. Eventually he worked out that something was amiss and some kinder person than we were removed them. I had a lot of fun with Alison Grant the music librarian too. For about a year we wrote an ongoing and ribald story on catalogue cards which concerned a wanton harlot called Persephone who indulged in salacious and lustful activities with strong manly strangers. We had turns writing a chapter and after a while we had a thick pile of these cards. I do not know what happened but they probably were thrown in a rubbish bin where they belonged.

During my time at the Wellington Public Library the Beatles came to Wellington on 21 June 1964. I was working in the Wellington Public Library. They were staying at the St George Hotel on the corner of Willis Street and Boulcott Street. This was just around the corner from the Wellington Public Library which they drove past as they came from the airport. Hysterical fans lined the route but I was not one of them. I had only ever been interested in classical music and had little exposure to anything else, mainly due to lack of interest but also lack of availability, although if there had been any enthusiasm one could easily seek out anything. I did stand at the window in the Reference Room on the first floor and watched as they glided past I but did not join the pulsating throngs out on the lawn in front of the library. I have never been a person to join in group adulation whether it be a musician, a celebrity of any sort, or a political person. I have done my share of demonstrating against issues, usually because I feel compelled to, but I do not enjoy mass action and feel uncomfortable and out of sorts in such activities. The first record I ever bought was Glenn Gould playing Bach *The Well-Tempered Clavier* and, although I had heard the Beatles, I was not drawn into their orbit at that time. I was drawn later as their timelessness, musicianship and their huge cultural influence eventually won me over.

Now Amelia and Fionn, while on the subject of Mr Silver, I have to recount to you another Flagpole moment which absolutely blighted my time at the Wellington Public library. Remember Flagpole moments are horrible things which 'come out of the blue' not slowly approaching things which build up to a horrible crescendo. It concerned Hildegard my scooter who had developed a puncture. The redoubtable Margaret Cavell and I removed the offending wheel from the scooter and carried it on the bus to the library. The plan was that I would take it in my lunch break over to the garage nearby. And this I did but it had unforeseen consequences I could never have imagined. There had been a series of thefts from our personal lockers which we had all been assigned in a special locker room. We each had our own locker with a key. Unbeknown to any of us the redoubtable Mr Silver had called in the police who had set up a trap using ultraviolet thief detection powder. A locker had been painted with this stuff and a key with an empty wallet placed inside to await the thief.

When I took Hildegard's wheel over to the garage I shut my locker but left the key in the lock as there was nothing inside. I was sitting quietly at my desk when the unctuous Mr Silver came sidling up to me. 'Miss Dowling, come with me'. Up I got eagerly thinking he was going to ask me to do some extra little task outside my usual duties. He took me into his room and sitting behind his desk were two policemen. 'Sit down' they said. Up went the flag to the top of the pole and I started to shake.

'We have reason to believe that you have been stealing money from the staff lockers'. I stared in disbelief and horror. These people had no idea about me. I absolutely believed at that time that if I stole the smallest item I would be cast into the depth of hell for all eternity. This fear and belief was absolutely etched on my consciousness. My fear of hell was strong and real. I had been programmed to take sixpence to the police station if I found it on the footpath. 'Please put out your hands' they asked me. Dumbly I did so. They shone an ultraviolet light on my hands and a muffled exchange took place between them. I was in a state of shock and was sure that at any moment I would wake up from this nightmare. 'Thank you Miss Dowling' said Mr Silver. 'You can go now'.

I left that room and like a zombie returned to my desk. I sat there staring into space not knowing what to do next. I phoned Margaret Cavell who came rushing to my side. Her outrage knew no bounds and her passionate expostulations in my defence were long and loud. How I loved that girl. She had such a straightforward sense of justice. She summoned Helen Burbery to my side. Up came Helen who boomed out her outrage and together they stood beside me vowing and declaring that this miscarriage of justice would not go unchallenged. I was an emotional wreck and there was no chance that I could do any more work. Margaret apprised her boss Alison Grant of the situation and asked if she could take me home which she did. At home in between deluges of weeping I tried to fathom what had happened and how I could be thus accused. After several hours and many cups of tea it dawned on me what had happened.

When I had taken Hildegard's wheel to the garage the thief had fallen for the planted trap thus covering her hands in the invisible powder. She had then seen my locker with the key in it and had turned the key and opened the locker only to find it empty. When I had returned from the garage I had put my valuables back in the locker and locked it thus transferring traces of the powder to my hands. When the police studied the lockers after the theft of the main plant they had also seen something on my locker.

The next day wild horses would not have succeeded in getting me back to the library. Margaret absolutely insisted and begged me to come back pointing out that my absence would give credence to my guilt so back I went flanked by Margaret. I can remember to this day walking up the steps of the library the day after flanked by Helen Burbery, Adrian Yska and Michael Wolliscroft. They met me at the door and together escorted me up to the Reference Room and all went in a group to express their horror at this accusation to Mr Silver. His room had been restored to its usual state. He told them that I had been eliminated as the powder on my hands was minimal, but the operation had been a failure and no one had been caught. We all thought we knew who it was but did not voice our suspicions. My support team demanded that Mr Silver apologise to me which he did half-heartedly. That man could not as the saying goes have organised 'a pissup in a brewery'. His ineptitude was profound but had horrible consequences for me.

The library had a lot of staff and by and large their support for me was muted as most of them did not know me. My brother Tony who was working as a lawyer for the Public Trust was horrified by what had happen. He had rushed to my side in his red Citroen and assured me that he would advocate for me with the city librarian Mr Perry which he did. Mr Perry got a bit nervous as my Uncle Ro was a City Councillor so he was in fact one of Mr Perry's bosses as the City Librarian had to account to the Wellington City Councillors for his management of the library. For weeks afterwards Margaret and Helen stood by my side when they could. I never went back to the tearoom for the rest of my tenure at the library as I could not face the stares and possible whispers. Fortunately I already had a plan to go to London three months after this happened so I knew I just had to weather the storm but the trauma remained for all that time.

As I write this I can feel the welling up of those feelings felt so long ago but I also remember the kindness and passion of my friends and my brother Tony. This experience also served to give me an acute response to injustice and false accusations which many people have endured. This story is 'small change' compared to the horrible miscarriages of justice that have occurred to countless people even to the extent of being executed for crimes they did not commit. Knowing that I was leaving New Zealand in the next three months was also a consolation. Mr Perry gave me a glowing reference which helped me in London. I had been a good and conscientious employee in any job I had undertaken thus far and continued to be for the rest of my working life.

Thus Amelia and Fionn, I terminated my tenure with the Wellington Public Library at the end of 1967 and went to Palmerston North to prepare for my departure to London in January 1968. It had by and large been a great experience apart from the events related above.

Chapter 15 – Back to my School Years.

Dear Amelia and Fionn:

I broke off earlier just as I was reaching my secondary school years so to this time I will now return. I left St Patrick's in Fitchett Street in Palmerston North when I had just turned thirteen and crossed the road to attend St Joseph's secondary school. Despite being thirteen I was very young both physically and mentally for my age and it was about this time I entered a very painful and self-conscious period. The year was 1958. There was only one look and that was blond, freckle-free, preferably with curly hair and flawless pale skin and a short and slightly turned up nose. I was the antithesis of this and believed with all my heart that I was ugly. The blueprints for our times were Debbie Reynolds and Doris Day. We only knew about them from films but such saccharine films were the fodder of the day and we swallowed them eagerly.

I remember my self- conscious phase vividly and it invaded every part of my life and imbued all the interactions I had with other people except my friends. It involved an intense reaction to any verbal encounters and any questions which took me by surprise. It was especially painful in church and coming back to my seat after going to the communion rails was a nightmare, as I was absolutely positive that I was going to get lost and miss my spot. There were so many landmarks in the form of my family taking up nearly a whole pew that it is surprising that this anxiety took hold.

By far the worst fear was that my nylons were suddenly going to slither down my legs and land at my feet on the way back from communion. They were held up by a tenuous and uncomfortable contraption called a suspender belt the components of which could suddenly snap releasing the top of the nylons they were holding up. Each nylon was held up by at least two of these so there was some insurance against this happening. If one gave way the nylons immediately wrinkled up around one's leg, which was an unforgiveable fashion crime. In our household one grabbed what one could by way of bodily garments and often too much had been asked of the elastic in the suspender belts so that

146

they were under some considerable strain to do their job properly. Being the fourth girl in a row many of these garments had already served beyond their expected tenure and should have been consigned to the scrap heap. Hence my anxiety fixated on those two potential disasters, wrinkled nylons or the worse horror nylons gathered around my ankles. Then there was the other great fear and that was the seams in the nylons which had to be straight. 'Are my seams straight?' was often heard in our household as crooked seams was an unacceptable fashion misdemeanour.

And so the anxieties piled up in my early teen age mind. *Kintho* had not worked so my freckles were back in full force and to top off the list of disadvantages I wore glasses and had done so since the age of nine. I still cried at the drop of a hat so the windscreen wipers were also doing overtime. My mother was often heard to say 'leave Susie. She's the sensitive one' or 'leave Susie, she's on penicillin.' This did not go down well with the perch dwellers as of course they too were sensitive but manifesting in different ways. My weeping was not as might be thought manipulative. It was just what I did in response to any adverse remarks or event. The floodgates were up and running and ready to burst open at any time. By far the worse reaction was blushing which I did all the time especially if pounced upon unexpectedly. This went on for many years in certain circumstances and I hated it but had no means of controlling it. It was at its worst when I was in a group and was asked a question and several pairs of eyes turned to look at me expecting an answer. My urge was to get up and run away but this was usually impossible so I had to sit it out and deal with it. Its genesis was great anxiety which over the years had grown to be a huge part of my life.

So I did not have 'the face that launched a thousand ships' as I entered secondary school with my friends in tow to do some serious learning. There we were divided into the two groups called Professional and Commercial as I have already related. I spent two years at St Joseph's and I might as well have been working behind the counter in Woolworths as the amount of learning I did was non-existent. In addition I did not try at all as the subject matter did not capture my attention. The first teachers I had were Sister Antonia and sometimes Sister Thomas. Under them there was no fear. Of course the terrifying music lessons under Sister Sophie continued unabated. Sister Antonia was young and attractive which even with all the paraphernalia they wore could be seen. She had beautiful creamy skin and soft brown eyes. It seemed to me that she always seemed to be a bit frightened and certainly if there was misbehaviour or insubordination she grew hot and bothered and tried to sound authoritative but never could.

Sister Thomas had had a stroke at a young age which had left her limbs, especially her hands, a bit floppy. She was always struggling with us as she had absolutely no discipline or authority at all. I wince now at the way we teased this poor woman as she tried to make us interested in 'The March of Civilisation' a horrible dry green covered book whose contents bore absolutely no relation to our lives. She also taught the sixth form Latin in the same room and at the same time as she was trying to teach us History. We sat on one side of the room and the sixth form sat on the other. She would assign us a few pages of the green book to read while she turned to attend to the Latin lesson. The windows of this room reached down to the top of our desks and there were capacious curtains. In summer the curtains were firmly pushed to the side and all the windows were wide open. As she was conjugating verbs with the 6th form we would draw the curtains over the window and quietly climb out the windows and disappear into the garden beside the classroom. When she turned to us leaving the sixth form with some task she would find no one there and the capacious curtains draped over our desks. 'Third form' she would cry plaintively 'come back at once' but by then we were out of earshot and nowhere to be seen.

I feel mean about the way we treated this poor woman but, in our defence, I have to say although she was one of the cleverest nuns with an MA in History but she was no teacher and we were all bored beyond belief. As a result my report at the end of the third form was so bad that I tore it up and threw it in the rubbish bin. My mother had so many other reports to read that she didn't miss mine. As a result of this bad report I added dumb to my list of personal attributes. When I was fourteen one of Phillippa's friends, who was also a novice nun, was talking to my mother. Suddenly she looked at me and said 'Susie, you have a chest like a scrubbing board'. At that stage any evidence that I belonged to the female sex was hard to detect but this remark cut me like a knife. This particular person herself was amply endowed. And so I added scrubbing board

148

chest to my list of deficiencies. Of course years later I managed to provide all the nourishment a small human being required from this 'scrubbing board', for two whole years which I hope Amelia has set you up well for life. Lots of people disapproved of breast-feeding for so long but I knew it was the right thing to do especially as the supply was copious and the demand from a small child was strong. Later, my friend Sue Girling-Butcher's father, who was a doctor, witnessed me in the act of breast-feeding. 'Do that as long as you can' he advised. "You are lining her stomach with health benefits which will last her for life'. But I have severely digressed so back to my school years.

Suddenly in the 4th form things improved. Sister Sophie disappeared and Sister Michelle took her place. I have already extolled her virtues above but suddenly learning the piano became enjoyable. She also trained the choir. She taught us good things and we had lots of fun. With Sister Sophie one quaked and quailed waiting for an outburst of rage. Once someone was singing out of tune and she turned to me and told me to stop singing. I was mortified beyond belief. If there was one talent I had it was singing in tune and I could not believe that this woman could not recollect the almost full marks I always got in the ear test part of the many music exams I had sat under her tutelage. The culprit was Helen Morpeth who was standing right next to me and was completely tone deaf. Helen stopped singing too so Sister Sophie thought she was had found the culprit.

I also had a teacher I liked called Sister Judith. She was the niece of Sister Elizabeth who had taught me in Standard 3 when I was nine and whose influence stays with me today. Sister Judith had a highly developed sense of fun but she was mercurial and had a nervy disposition so the weather could change quickly. She was not averse to using the strap but not very convincingly. She never touched me and at this point it is probably relevant to say that I was never ever strapped during my whole my school career while others around me were. My father never hit me either which remains a mystery to this day. My only conclusion is that they sensed the readiness of the waterworks which along with the windscreen wipers were ready to jump to. I do not know what it is, but I have never ever been hit by any adult in my entire life. Maybe I have made the 'stricken look' into an art form which causes the perpetrator of the corporal punishment to desist.

Sister Judith was a good teacher but despite her attempts I did badly in the 4th form but I did have a lot of fun. Helen Morpeth was writing plays and giving me the lead role. We had Vocation Day and I came to school dressed as a Sister of Mercy. I did well in my Grade 5 music exam and theory exam. Sister Judith once heard me singing fake falsetto which I was good at. When she was bored she would call me up to the front of the class and command me to sing 'I could have danced all night' which I did with gusto. She loved this and would laugh uncontrollably. The rest of the class listened but do not think they derived the pleasure from it which she did.

Again, at the end of the year, I got a better report but it was still not good so into the rubbish bin it went. The head nun at St Joseph's was Sister Mechtilde. She was part of a family dynasty who had supplied the Sisters of Mercy with three nuns who were all verging on being dwarfs, all below five feet tall. I had little to do with her but she enraged my father by forbidding Phillipa to sit school certificate because she claimed she would not pass. My father stormed up to the school and did battle with this small person to no avail. During my time at St Joseph's I played tennis and basketball incessantly and absolutely loved it. I was always in the top teams as were all my sisters. Margaret was an excellent player and was chosen to be a Palmerston North Representative chosen from all the schools in the city and district. I was never as good as my other sisters but was perfectly happy with my performance and the pleasure I derived from it.

During this time at St Joseph's I had befriended Bernadette Black. She was an orphan and had been adopted by Mr and Mrs Black. We became friends as Bernadette was eventually taken in by my mother's friend and fellow 6am mass attendee Mrs O'Keefe. As she became a teenager, she had become too much for the Black's as she matured quickly and maybe started to become insubordinate so Mrs O'Keefe took her in even though she already had five children of her own. Had she foreseen the antics of Bernardette and her son Maurice she might have demurred but I kept my counsel in this matter. Bernadette was a very good tennis player and we played as much as we could. She was great fun but could be sulky and moody and not talk to me for several days so when we were in the tennis finals and she was my opponent I let her win as I feared the silent backlash she was so good at.

The O'Keefes lived in Annandale Avenue, around the corner from us, and she and my mother had become firm friends as they were both frenetic in the practice of their religion. Mrs O'Keefe was a convert and had embraced the faith with a fervour and obsession sometimes seen in such people. She found a ready confrere in my mother and together they attended 6am Mass in the parish of Shamrock Street every single morning. She was always eager to convert other people and had a lot of success with this enterprise. She was a consummate businesswoman and had a thriving hairdressing business which eventually my sister Margaret was employed in after she left school and before leaving to live in Australia. Mrs O'Keefe set about converting her staff and succeeded with her chief hairdresser called Athlene. I do not know how much coercion went on but Mrs O'Keefe was a strong and determined woman when it came to converting people. She was driven and when she smiled her face did not show delight or pleasure but was more of a rictus smile. My father was not keen on her at all and constantly referred to her as the 'tax dodger' as she had purchased some land on Norfolk Island which in his opinion was a way of avoiding tax.

After the Cowan family moved from Gisborne to Palmerston North and moved next door to the O'Keefe's she set about working on Mrs Cowan who was not a Catholic but had married one. Mrs Cowan had enough going on with the reality of Johnny and the difficulties associated with dealing with him and eventually collapsed with a nervous breakdown which was not at all surprising as she was a sensitive woman and perhaps the pressure of 'conversion' was the' final straw which broke the camel's back'. This is all conjecture on my part it must be conceded.

There was also a person called Tom Stanley who Mrs O'Keefe had taken under her wing. I know little about him but I think he was what people call a 'lost soul' so she got out her conversion toolkit and very soon he was being baptised and confirmed. Tom Stanley was tall and good looking but there was something about him which gave cause for pause. Today one would pick up quickly if a person was homosexual and it would be no issue whatsoever, but then I didn't even know the word and there was certainly no consideration of this but that's probably what Tom Stanley was at a time when the closet doors were not only shut but firmly bolted and barred. In the fullness of time Tom Stanley spied my handsome brother Rolly and by some machinations unknown to me took him by car to Taupo. To this day no one knows what, if anything, happened but Rolly tried to escape. Whether successfully or not I do not know as my knowledge of this event is sketchy. Years later Tom Stanley was convicted of some misdemeanour with a boy in Palmerston North and the story made the headlines of the *Manawatu Evening Standard*.

I am probably trying to explain based on rather flimsy evidence why my brother Rolly became the person he is today, virtually a recluse who spurns most family encounters and leads a solitary life tending his garden. He has my father's green fingers. When he was born he was the first boy after a string of four 'bloody girls' and he was much favoured by my father and even taken to work with him in the green van and he was probably given extra Foxton Fizz when the rest of us weren't looking. So the puzzle remains. He sat on the perch below me and in the fullness of time managed to lean up and peck me unmercifully. Later when my mother was deep in her mental illness he was sent to the Marist Brothers' novitiate at Tuakau when he was only 13 or 14, so who knows what went on there. This was a time when children had to be shed because there was no end in sight for a recovery and it had become untenable for me to carry on as chief cook and bottlewasher. Lucy was sent to board at St Mary's and Joseph to board at St Joseph's in Masterton.

Rolly did not become a Marist Brother and has never divulged anything at all concerning anything untoward, so the mystery remains. He went on to gain a degree in food technology. There was one incident concerning Rolly which I will never forget. He had shoplifted in Woolworths and because of this a police car arrived at our house. This was the greatest shame imaginable for my parents who were absolute upholders of honesty and clung tenaciously to high standards of morality not to mention their strict adherence to the fifth commandment 'Thou shalt not steal'. Rolly admitted to his crime and for the first time ever I heard my mother say 'Wait until your father comes home'. When my father did come home Rolly was subjected to a long beating. We all stood around crying and begging him to stop. I actually believe my father did not like doing this and it never happened again. He was much more a man of the moment in his anger but this time he had to summon it to order. This was a horrible event and rare, I am glad to say.

Chapter 16 - St Mary's

Dear Amelia and Fionn:

I have severely digressed Amelia and Fionn: from my two years of secondary school at St Joseph's, but Bernadette Black sent lots of memories flooding back which I felt compelled to relate. I left St Joseph's at the end of the 4th form and the next year headed to boarding school at St Mary's in Wellington. By this time I was fifteen. My mother was in a terrible way but still clinging on and managing the house and looking after the 'three little ones'.

At first I was homesick as by that time I had made homesickness into an art form. I constantly worried about my mother and when I went home for the holidays there was the relentless pursuit from room to room with the repetitive catalogue of her worries. Desperation was mounting as medical solutions had been an abysmal failure. My father was having a horrible time as increasingly he had to take on the domestic chores as my mother became worse and worse. The poor woman was severely tormented and this troubled me a great deal. Meantime I was set down in a new school with a new set of friends to make. My sister Pauline was in the 7th form but had to become a day girl so that my fees could be afforded, so she lived with my grandmother doubling as a boarder and slave. There was a chance that she was to be appointed Head Girl but she had ruined those chances in the 6th form when they were assigned to write a limerick. One of the lines in her limerick was 'she was aye a virgin at seventeen, a remarkable thing in Aberdeen'. Eyes narrowed, lips pursed, teeth were sucked in and demotion decreed. The shock and horror at such wickedness blew all her chances of this honour. She was far more of an all-rounder and leader than the person called Geraldine Dawrick whom they did appoint. My sister Phillippa had entered the convent so was also at St Mary's serving her novitiate so there were a few familiar faces around.

Coming in at the 5th form meant that people's friendships had already been established so I would have to permeate some solid friendship walls which I did quite quickly. I befriended Catherine Furness who came from Blenheim. Catherin was an open and friendly person who also happened to be beautiful. She had the most stunning blue eyes with the longest eye lashes I have ever seen to this day. Despite this she was humble and even-tempered and had a deeply empathetic nature. We became firm friends quickly and she invited me to Blenheim in the August school holidays which I readily accepted. The Furness family home was quiet and peaceful with no tensions or outbursts of any kind. Mr Furness was dis not say much and Mrs Furness welcomed me warmly. Apart from Mary's family this was the first time as an adult I had witnessed another family who were not related in their domestic environment and I can tell you it provided a strong contrast to mine.

Later Catherine Furness came to stay with us and I lived in a state of abject terror that she would be overwhelmed by the domestic thunder and lightning which she wasn't. She just giggled nervously when it broke out or I desperately tried to camouflage by singing or talking loudly. The fashion then was to wear sloppy loose fitting jerseys and by some miracle I had knitted myself one at boarding school where help was to hand. The adjunct to this fashion item was a paisley scarf knotted rakishly around one's neck. It too had to hang loosely. Catherine had all the necessary garments but I lacked the scarf component. So I sneaked into Margaret's drawer and stole one as she was at work. After our bike ride I took out the iron in order to iron out the creases and return it to its place. But alas the iron was too hot and I put a huge hole in it. What to do and what I did does not reflect well on me. I folded it carefully and returned it to the drawer hoping that it would not be the scarf of choice for some time to come. Of course Margaret did discover it but her reaction was fairly muted as I promised to replace it as soon as I could. I don't think I ever did.

I was assigned to Form 5A as they assumed that I would be clever because Pauline was, and I was Sister Campion's niece and she had a university degree in English which wasn't that usual amongst our teachers although it was more common at St Mary's. I completely floundered in 5A due largely to my slow development and my complete lack of diligence in Forms 3 and 4 at St Joseph's. I was being taught things in biology I had never heard of. History was a complete mystery due to my eschewing of 'The March of Civilisation'. The word Europe

155

kept being mentioned in our history lessons but the school environment did not invite any enquiry and I had no idea what Europe was and was too scared to ask in case everyone else knew and I would be laughed at.

So I made a strong resolution that when I could I would go there and find out where and what Europe was for myself and this I did. I responded to English as that was my natural haven. As already described, School Certificate Music was way beyond my ken. I was always anxious largely due to the mystery of what was happening to my mother. This reached a crescendo at one point that I started walking in my sleep and on several occasions was found at the foot of the stairs starting to don my hat and coat saying 'I'm going to get my mother'. No help or guidance let alone reassurance was offered so I soldiered on. Finally in desperation I went to see Sister Monica who was my form teacher and begged to be put in a lower fifth form. She listened kindly and politely but would not oblige.

My anxiety reached a crescendo when Sister Matthew was teaching us biology. She was a stern forbidding person who had a habit of pouncing on any class member with some question pertaining to the subject. I would sit there terrified clinging under the desk to the hand of a wonderful girl called Glenis Eady who sat next to me. She was clever and always knew the answers. If I was ever pounced on she would try either to whisper the answer or write it on a piece of paper which she had to the ready under the desk in big letters so that I could read it. To give Sister Matthew her due I think she saw the abject terror on my face which by now was my default position whenever danger threatened. She started to leave me alone but I never relaxed as I never knew when a pounce was imminent.

And so I got through the 5th form and just passed School Certificate. When the results plopped into the letterbox at 35 Beresford Street I retrieved them eagerly, tore them open and was greatly relieved that I had got 246 for my four subjects. 200 was a pass so I was happy with that as to fail in our family wasn't an option and would only reinforce my belief that I was as thick as two short planks. My mother was in such a dark state of despair that I did not tell her or anyone. In the same manner as School reports weren't missed this also was not noticed.

156

During these holidays my friend Joan Walters from school in Palmerston North and I had planned a trip to the South Island. We had decided to call on the various relations scattered around the West Coast and see Olive and Mrs Knox in Christchurch catching trains and busses as we went. In retrospect I look back on this as quite a plucky enterprise and wonder if all those relatives were so enamoured by the intrusion of a random niece and her friend. However, they were all kind and welcoming. Down at the Inangahua Junction where my mother's brother Uncle Pat lived, we met endless numbers of cousins most of whom I have never seen since. Aunty Helen was Uncle Pat's wife and they had eight children. She was my godmother a role she more or less ignored having enough on her hands in the form of dependents. My godfather was her son Jim but as far as I know no one told him as there was no acknowledgment of the role which did not concern me at all.

Olive and Mrs Knox need some discussion and amplification as they played an important role in our family's life in the Christchurch Days. As I was only two when we left there most of the information I have is hearsay. The first thing to say is that they were not Catholics but were Brethren. The fact that they were allowed to 'penetrate the ramparts' and permeate our family says a great deal about them. Mrs Knox came in as to help my overwhelmed mother. My suspicion is that my grandmother paid for this as I do not think my father's salary allowed for paid domestic help however desperately needed. They were nice, kind generous people and became family friends. Olive knitted the most amazing garments and we can still see the matching jerseys she knitted in family photographs. I think Olive and Mrs Knox became attached to us and even after we moved to Palmerston North they would come and stay. Olive was a large person who had been bullied at school because of it. She would recount the taunt of 'Olive Polive stick stack stolive, hi bomb chickerbom, fat old Olive'. I hated to hear this but it was her reality so she never ventured far from her mother's side and never left home. Olive would not have harmed anyone but had limited her horizons because of the bullying and a generally timid disposition. I adored Olive and when they stayed I would climb into bed with her in the morning and snuggle down into her ample bosom which she did not seem to mind. She used to call me 'wee Sue' as I was still the youngest when they first came to stay.

And so Amelia and Fionn, after that short digression I will return to my school days at St Mary's. I entered the 6th form and was greatly relieved not to be taught anything by Sister Matthew. Sister Dominic was my class teacher and although solemn and serious she was nevertheless kind and well-disposed and I liked her a lot. Sister Marcia taught me English. She was a lively intelligent person who taught us interesting things such as 'The Waste Land' by TS Eliot. Although I did not have a clue what she was talking about I responded at that other intuitive level to the language and loved it. It was the same response I had had at the age of nine with Sister Elizabeth where comprehension was absent but appreciation was absolute. Who could not respond to words such as 'What are the roots that clutch, what branches grow out of this stony rubbish' and' Phlebas the Phoenician, a fortnight dead forgot the cry of the gulls and the deep sea swell and the profit and loss' How could I have ever known that years later I would perform in a dramatised version directed by Michael Hurst for the Auckland Theatre Company. What's more, I was allowed to utter those wonderful immortal words

April is the cruellest month,

breeding lilacs out of the dead land,

mixing memory and desire,

stirring dull roots with spring rain.

How could I have ever known that the obscure meaning of this work would become comprehensible to me and that I would commit large tracts of it to memory. Such are the mysteries of life.

The sixth form was a hard slog to try and get accredited at the end and not have to sit the University Entrance exam. By this time I was performing reasonably well and certainly studying hard. I was also playing a great deal of basketball and tennis which I loved. Boarding school life had settled down but my mother was still ill and a constant source of worry. The boarder's mistress was Sister de Sales. She was not popular and did not have the common touch at all. I think the general consensus was that she was false and she certainly fawned a great deal over any priest who came on weekly visits to the boarding school. The highlight of the year was the Boarders vs Day Scholars basketball tournament. I was in the Boarders' team and Pauline was in the Day

Scholars' team and as luck would have it. Pauline was a formidable defence and she always seemed stronger and more powerful than I was so I had to dart nimbly around to avoid her.

I was in the goal shooters ring and Pauline was my partner as goal attack. My sister Philippa was the referee so it was quite a family affair. I have no recollection who won in the year this happened but I do recall that it was great fun and I loved it. The whole day was devoted to it and we sang songs which we had been made up by us and former students long gone. We sang with great gusto to the tunes of popular tunes already in existence. One I recall was to the tune of Finiculi Funicula. It's banality hits me today but lustily we sang

Christopher Columbus what do you think of that?

The boarders will conquer the day girls 'til they're flat,

So come on blue we'll cheer for you, you know we will not rest at all.

Until the cup is once again safe in the social hall.

The social hall was a large room where all the boarders gathered at the end of the day to dance to the popular tunes of the day. This was after our evening meal and two hours of study. It was during this time that I learned a lot of the popular hit tunes of the day. There was always a nun on duty making sure we did not do anything lewd in response to this decadent music, but in general I enjoyed these sessions and was pleased to be able to tune in to the current hits. We were able to practise for the school dance which was an annual event for Forms 6 and 7.

I dreaded events such as this as I never seemed to have the right attire and I knew that I would probably be what was then called a 'wall flower' unless there was a boy in attendance with an equal portion of low self esteem and would feel as inadequate as I felt and we would possibly find our match. Usually such people couldn't dance to save themselves and due to my natural sense of rhythm and lots of practice in the social hall I could dance so would have to endure much standing on toes and quite a few collisions with other dancers. Sometimes there were dances held in the church hall in Palmerston North to which I would go usually because my friends were going. These were definitely torture as again I never liked the garment I had scraped together and watched while the

'Doris Days and Debbie Reynolds' lookalikes were not only snatched up quickly but actually competed for. Glasses, freckles and straight brown hair and a plate straightening my teeth did not really cut it on the dance floor. As a result the toilet was visited often where one encountered like persons escaping the mortification of rejection.

Fortunately Helen Morpeth was my companion in these events. She also had glasses, straight brown hair and to top off her list of crimes was really tall. She was by far the most interesting person I encountered in my school life but being incredibly original and talented did not cut it on the dance floor in Palmerston North in the dying days of the fifties. Still school dances were a chance to hear the popular music of the day which was distinctly discouraged in Beresford Street and as we only had by then one scratchy radio so any listening had to be clandestine and when my father was absent. If he did pass by due to some error of planning on our part he would say 'Turn that bloody noise off' and so we did.

After the Boarders – Day Scholars match the cup was presented to the victorious team and a hearty afternoon tea was devoured. All the catering was done by Sister Barbara and I can only imagine how tedious that job was. She was quite a dour person but had a merry twinkle on the odd occasion. She fed us well but there was a lot of bread involved and we all seemed to acquire what I call bread stomachs which is a slight pot which even I, with all my skinniness, had. I had made many friends by the sixth form especially amongst the boarders but also amongst the day girls. I became particularly close to a Tongan girl called Deanna Brown. She had an unquenchable sense of fun and such people drew me like a magnet.

Another girl called Kay Fowler I would look at with great pity and anguish as her mother had died which was why she had to become a boarder. She was beautiful and had a pale fragile look and always looked sad. I used to imagine what it would be like if one's mother died and could not dwell on that for long without a gush of horror coming upon me. I was always feeling sad about my mother and felt especially alone and fearful at night. There had been a prowler found lurking around the boarding school at night and this fed into and intensified my fear. I often lay wide awake half the night. Sometimes I would ask Catherine Furness if she minded if I crept in beside her if I was feeling particularly nervous.

Being the kindest and most sympathetic person in the world she always said yes to this and so sometimes I did.

One morning I was summoned into Sister de Sales's office and interrogated about this, which puzzled me a great deal as I had no idea what the sub plot was here. I had no idea what she was implying as I had never ever heard the word lesbian and had no idea that such people existed. This might sound hard to believe but it is absolutely true. My horizons were about as wide as a pencil and the input into my life was so limited that such realities did not exist to me. Remember that my reading matter was limited to religious tracts and journals which would never ever even contemplate canvassing topics such as these. I had been spied on and dobbed in by a particularly sneaky postulant with the unfortunate name of Sister Bonaventure. Her name was so inappropriate and she certainly did not seem to be having a good time at all and in retrospect I feel rather sorry for her as she looked decidedly unhappy. I have since discovered that she left the convent and let's hope that she's having better times. But she put paid to my seeking comfort during a difficult time for me. I had, from time to time at home, climbed into bed with my sister Pauline and certainly with 'Olive Polive stick stack stolive' as already recounted and thought it was a perfectly acceptable thing to do. It was years before the penny dropped and the subtext of Sister de Sales's unsavoury implications hit me.

I have already recounted the music in my life at St Mary's which I loved, apart from the 'Alla Turca' experience. I played tennis all the time and loved that. If we were in the middle of a game and the midday chapel bells tolled we had to drop our rackets and fall to our knees to recite the Angelus.

> *The Angel of the Lord declared unto Mary and she conceived of the Holy Spirit.*

When that was finished we resumed our game. There were other nuns I had little to do with but they were all nice to me. They included Sister Julian, Sister Emmanual and one we called 'Feather duster ' because she was never seen without one in her hand flicking away any speck of dust which landed near her. Her real name was Sister Marcel. Then there was Mother Gabrielle who was reputed to be 100 and she died while I was at boarding school. But during that year my mother's condition had deteriorated to the point that drastic action had to be taken so to Porirua Mental Hospital she had to go. All other courses of action had failed There were still three young children to be cared for so, as already recounted the obvious choice to fill the role was me. And fill it I did. I was sorry to say goodbye to my friends at St Mary's and knew that, apart from Catherine Furness, I would probably not see any of them again as they all lived in different parts of the country and two of them in the Pacific. This proved to be true and so to Palmerston North I headed with a heavy heart.

Chapter 17 - And so I Depart

Dear Amelia and Fionn:

I have already recounted the time I spent in Palmerston North and then my time in Wellington but as I bring this account to a close I realise that the timeline is all over the place but such things reflect the nature of life I believe so I now turn to my departure on the liner *Fairsky* on 9 January 1968. I was twenty two years and two months. When I was a young child I knew I wanted to travel. I knew at some sentient level that my horizons were rather limited and I knew I had to go and find out for myself, especially where Europe was. I had not finished my Library Certificate but I threw caution to the wind anyway. I was armed with good references from Miss Green from the library in Palmerston North and Mr Perry from the Wellington Public Library which showed that I was a good conscientious worker and in both libraries had been promoted quickly to responsible positions.

I had no idea what lay in store for me in London but I felt sure I would get a job and was prepared to do anything and this proved to be true. I also had the consoling knowledge that my friend Randall McMullen was there as was Graham Parsons and of course Alison Lee. Randall was not the good friend he was to become but he was a connection and a good solid one at that and, although I didn't know it then, we had already met when I was eight and he was nine at St Madeleine Sophie's school in Island Bay. I would travel up from Southampton where the boat docked in the company, as it turned out, of the many people I had met on the boat. Randall had promised to meet me from the train at Waterloo in London and said that I could stay with him and Graham Parsons in his flat in Cricklewood.

And so I boarded the *Fairsky*. Below me were lots of people seeing me off, in fact a sea of faces including four nuns who had taught me at St Mary's. My overriding feeling was not of excitement but great relief. I had to escape from the proximity of my mother's torment and as I gazed down I saw that face in the crowd, hollowed out, lifeless and the marks of mental torture written all over it. She had said to me a few months earlier

'Susie I would end it all if I wasn't going to go to hell'. I probably replied 'mum, you are in hell'. By then I knew I had no answers and never had had but being human I had tried so hard to 'jolly her out' of her obsessions. It was going to take more than that of course it did take more than that. Early in 1970 she had her first leucotomy and a second in August 1971 but of course I was far, far away and grateful for it. After the second one she did get a lot of relief but I was not there to see it.

In fact this procedure must have removed lots of filters as she became more brazen and would say things she never would have said before. For example, once in church and I think it was at my Brother Dermot's profession as a Marist Brother she called out in a loud voice 'You're a fraud.' This remark was directed at the Priest on the altar and was an unthinkable prospect in the days when she was gripped by her mental illness. She would often say audibly 'He's a goat' within the hearing of the person being so named.

She wrote to me twice in nearly five years so I relied on the generous outpourings of my sister MaryClare to keep up with the news. Once a blue aerogramme plopped into my letterbox and I saw with great excitement that it bore my mother's hand. She always put SAG on the back of all her correspondence which stood for 'Saint Anthony Guide' and there it was. Saint Anthony certainly had guided it safely to my letterbox and I tore it open excitedly. The blue aerogramme was absolutely blank. Not one word was written on this blue sheet. I stared in disbelief but I absolutely knew that behind this was nothing but good intentions. There was absolutely no malice in my mother. She had simply thought she had filled it with words but she had not. So absent-mindedly she had sealed it and put it in the letterbox.

I had made lots of clothes to take on my journey so with Margaret Cavell many visits were made to Thomson's Silk shop in Willis Street where with Margaret's help I bought lots of material which she helped me turn into garments. There were many more encounters with 'make up real smart' of course. One of the fabrics was a striped dark green, a lighter green and a cream stripe. The pattern was like a sailor's outfit with a large front flap and short sleeves and I thought this dress was just the ticket for the nautical experience I was about to have. As the ship's horn boomed out and the ship glided away from the dock, the crowd below started to disperse. As I watched them depart I do not know what went through my mind and I stood at the rail for a long time watching them recede. I had already investigated my cabin and deposited my luggage but had not as yet met my cabin mates as they like me were busy waving and throwing streamers to the crowd below. Once there was some distance from the wharf I sank exhaustedly into the nearest deck chair. Suddenly I realised that the deck chair I had sunk into with great relief 'made up real smart' too. For although it was made of stouter fabric I stared in horror when I saw that my dress and the deck chair were made of the same colours.

THE END

Epilogue

26 July 2021

Dear Amelia and Fionn:

Well, I did it! I hope you now know quite a lot more about me than you did before you read this narrative.

Sometimes it was not easy to recount certain things and other times I found myself highly entertained. I hope you and any other readers find some parts a little sobering but in equal proportion are amused by other segments

My childhood was I think, quite unusual. Not many people I know, have so many brothers and sisters and consequently so many nieces and nephews and now so many grown up great nieces and nephews. I think I am lucky to be able to dip into this rich source; and dip into it I do. There is not one dud among them. They are all highly intelligent, interesting and have strong moral and ethical standards which they apply to their lives. My life is definitely enriched by them.

I was affected adversely for some time by parts of my childhood, especially my mother's mental illness. For many years there seemed to be no glimmer of light anywhere on the horizon. These events certainly sucked the laugh out of me for a few years and I remember this strongly. I could not laugh robustly and out loud for a long time. That has now all changed and I laugh a lot.

For a long time I did think I was a 'useless article' and a 'nuisance'. But those thoughts have long gone and now in 2021 I feel loved and valued especially by my friends and family. I have a strong sense of my point of view and sometimes express it vociferously, Maybe I am making up for lost time.

There could be a Volume Two of these letters, but I am not promising anything.

Your loving mother and grandmother
Suzanne Frances Dowling

www.ingramcontent.com/pod-product-compliance
Lightning Source LLC
Chambersburg PA
CBHW072007040426
42447CB00009B/1527